WBCA
Offensive Plays
& Strategies

WOMEN'S BASKETBALL
COACHES ASSOCIATION
WBCA

Beth Bass, CEO
Betty Jaynes, Consultant

Human Kinetics

Library of Congress Cataloging-in-Publication Data

WBCA offensive plays & strategies / Women's Basketball Coaches Association.
   p. cm.
  ISBN-13: 978-0-7360-8731-5 (softcover)
  ISBN-10: 0-7360-8731-1 (softcover)
 1. Basketball--Offense. 2. Basketball for women. 3. Basketball--Coaching. I. Women's Basketball Coaches Association. II. Title: WBCA offensive plays and strategies.
  GV889.W38 2011
  796.323'2--dc22

2011004872

ISBN-10: 0-7360-8731-1 (print)
ISBN-13: 978-0-7360-8731-5 (print)

Copyright © 2011 by Women's Basketball Coaches Association

Acquisitions Editor: Justin Klug
Developmental Editor: Kevin Matz
Assistant Editor: Steven Calderwood
Copyeditor: John Wentworth
Graphic Designer: Joe Buck
Graphic Artist: Francine Hamerski
Cover Designer: Keith Blomberg
Art Manager: Kelly Hendren
Associate Art Manager: Alan L. Wilborn
Illustrations: © Human Kinetics
Printer: McNaughton & Gunn, Inc.

Special thanks to Jana Hunter for her contributions to the manuscript.

Human Kinetics books are available at special discounts for bulk purchase. Special editions or book excerpts can also be created to specification. For details, contact the Special Sales Manager at Human Kinetics.

Printed in the United States of America   10 9 8 7 6 5 4 3 2 1

The paper in this book is certified under a sustainable forestry program.

Human Kinetics
Website: www.HumanKinetics.com

United States: Human Kinetics
P.O. Box 5076
Champaign, IL 61825-5076
800-747-4457
e-mail: humank@hkusa.com

Canada: Human Kinetics
475 Devonshire Road Unit 100
Windsor, ON N8Y 2L5
800-465-7301 (in Canada only)
e-mail: info@hkcanada.com

Europe: Human Kinetics
107 Bradford Road
Stanningley
Leeds LS28 6AT, United Kingdom
+44 (0) 113 255 5665
e-mail: hk@hkeurope.com

Australia: Human Kinetics
57A Price Avenue
Lower Mitcham, South Australia 5062
08 8372 0999
e-mail: info@hkaustralia.com

New Zealand: Human Kinetics
P.O. Box 80
Torrens Park, South Australia 5062
0800 222 062
e-mail: info@hknewzealand.com

E4981

WBCA

Offensive Plays & Strategies

CONTENTS

Foreword vii ▌ Preface ix
Key to Diagrams xi

Chapter **1** The Game Plan 1

Chapter **2** Fast-Break Offense 17

Chapter **3** Post Plays vs. Man-to-Man Defense 61

Chapter **4** Perimeter Plays vs. Man-to-Man Defense 95

Chapter **5** Post Plays vs. Zone Defense 117

Chapter 6 Perimeter Plays vs. Zone Defense 147

Chapter 7 Out-of-Bounds Plays 173

Chapter 8 Beating the Press 207

Chapter 9 Quick-Shot Plays 221

About the WBCA 263 ❙ Contributors 265

FOREWORD

Basketball is a game that requires a strong blend of physical and mental skills. Players must be sound in its fundamentals—dribbling, shooting, and passing—before they can even begin to understand how to play the game. It's the tactical team skills, however, that are necessary for competing and winning at a high level. This book will help develop those tactical skills.

Offensive structure, presented in *WBCA Offensive Plays & Strategies*, is designed to create organization for your players. Each player will have a complete understanding of her responsibilities on the court, which will make every player quicker. A player can be decisive when she knows each teammate will do her part. This leads to chemistry and, therefore, successful team offense.

This book offers advice to both coaches and players. Coaches will learn the plays and strategies necessary for success. Players, meanwhile, will find advice to help them understand the demands of the game and their roles within the specific plays that coaches ask them to perform.

The plays presented in this book are designed by 25 of the finest coaches of women's basketball. All are members of the Women's Basketball Coaches Association (WBCA). Many are conference regular-season champions, conference tournament champions, and NCAA national champions. The plays are explained so that any coach, regardless of experience, can use them with players at any level.

One mission of the WBCA is to provide coaches with instructional resources that will contribute to their success. We as coaches should always look for ways to provide the information necessary to help our athletes come together and succeed as a team. This book goes a long way in providing that information.

Charli Turner Thorne
Head coach, women's basketball
Arizona State Sun Devils

PREFACE

WBCA Offensive Plays & Strategies combines the knowledge of 25 of the game's top coaches to give you the plays right from their own playbooks. With this book you'll not only have the plays themselves, but the insight and tips from the coaches who have mastered them on the game's biggest stage. *WBCA Offensive Plays & Strategies* offers coaches the information they need for devising the optimal offensive approach for their team and its success.

The *WBCA Offensive Plays & Strategies* provides guidance for every offensive situation in the game with 119 plays for scoring, inbounding the ball, breaking a defensive press, and many other situations a coach will encounter. It was written to present an insider's view of the best approaches to the offensive aspects of women's basketball. Coaches and players alike will find valuable guidance on the movements and tactics in the most effective offensive systems used in the game. The book also compares the plays—based on alignment and execution, personnel requirements, and unique advantages and disadvantages—so that coaches can match them up to make the best use of their team's talents and to fit specific opponents and situations.

Chapter 1 provides in-depth coverage of successful game planning, making sure your players are prepared for everything your opponent can throw at you. Next, you get plays designed specifically for a team running a fast-break offense. Then the book gives you post and perimeter plays designed for use against both zone and man-to-man coverage. Out-of-bounds plays and plays for beating the press are covered next. And finally quick-shot plays are presented, for those times when a quick score is needed.

Champions make the game look effortless, with every player operating in sync with the other, like pieces of an efficient, well-oiled machine. This book offers you a special collection of plays and coaching points from champion coaches to develop and hone individual and team performance on both ends of the court. Great team skills don't necessarily increase your chances of making the TV highlights, but they do make it much more likely that you'll cut down the nets at the end of the season.

KEY TO DIAGRAMS

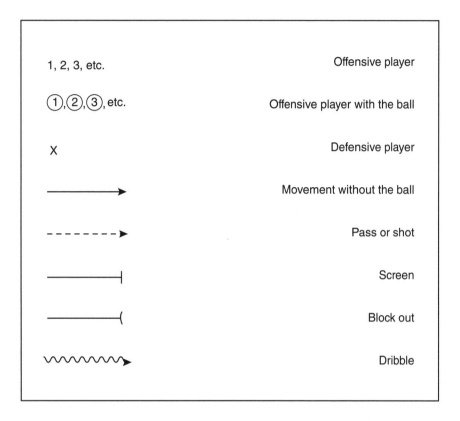

1, 2, 3, etc.	Offensive player
①, ②, ③, etc.	Offensive player with the ball
X	Defensive player
→	Movement without the ball
‑ ‑ ‑ ‑ ►	Pass or shot
⊢	Screen
⊣	Block out
∿∿∿►	Dribble

CHAPTER

1

The Game Plan

A major difference between a well-coached basketball game and a high-level pick-up game isn't so much in the style of play as in the planning and strategy that precedes the contest. The individual players on the blacktop might have more raw talent than the players in the high school gym, but getting a *team* ready to compete at the highest level requires a great deal of preparation from both coaches and players.

From what you hear on television, it might sound big-time to pour over your next opponent's offenses, defenses, and player strengths and weaknesses before spending hours of practice time on the court to ensure your team knows exactly how to respond to the opponent's every move, but the truth is that great teams spend much more time focusing on themselves—their own fundamentals, their own style, and their own plays—than they do on their opponents.

Many questions must be answered as your team develops its on-court identity: What tangible and intangible characteristics define your team? What type of offense will you run? What type of defense? Will you apply full-court pressure most of the game or only at critical times? Will your team thrive within a fast-breaking system, or is its strength a half-court game? Will your team take pride in rebounding, in defense, in being smart with the ball, or simply in scoring a lot of points? On what peg will your team hang its uniform?

The answers to these questions are the foundation of the coach's plan for how to maximize talent and minimize weaknesses. Teams with larger players normally tend toward a half-court game because they have the bulk to take up space inside the paint but lack the speed to play an up-tempo style. A small, quick team with good stamina may employ a full-court press most of the game, using its speed to create turnovers and its endurance to wear down the opponent. A team whose collective heart outweighs its raw talent often will play a hard-nosed, gritty brand of ball, scrapping for, hustling toward, and rebounding every ball. Though not necessarily recommended, one with several sharp shooters may bank on simply outscoring the other team rather than making defense and rebounding a priority.

Once those traits and tendencies are identified, the coach can set about creating a plan for the team. The plan covers everything from practice design and film sessions to play selection and game strategy. The length, intensity, and minute-by-minute schedule of practice will depend on details such as the team's current fitness level, the fitness level needed to execute the game plan, and the degree to which precision is critical to the team's success.

Once your team has chosen its desired identity, many months of dedicated practice are required to achieve that identity. A large part of a team's identity depends on the plays the team chooses to run. The collection of plays in a team's arsenal should directly complement its offensive strengths: half-court or fast-breaking style, post or perimeter play. Then plays specifically designed for various defenses can be honed based on the style of play of each opponent. For this book we have selected plays that the best collegiate women's basketball programs in the United States run regularly. We tell you which plays best apply to which situations based on game circumstances and personnel. For each play, we provide detailed, step-by-step instructions and diagrams to ensure the play will run as smoothly for your team as it does for the team that first created it.

As tempting as it might be to design your team's offensive sets on how an opponent defends, that is putting the cart before the horse. Only after a coach has evaluated a team's makeup and abilities, and after a team is comfortable and effective with its trademark traits and play sets, does it make sense to turn attention to the opponents.

Just as foolish as focusing too much attention on an opponent is paying no attention to them at all. Before you face an opponent you need to study and observe their tendencies so you can plan to counter them. How will your offense attack a team's full-court press? How will you handle their big bodies at the post? Their speed at the perimeter? Their all-out assault on the defensive boards?

Once you know an opponent's tendencies, when developing your game plan you can outline an approach to take against the opponent, replacing unknowns with specifics to give your players a mental and physical advantage. In forming your game plan you break an abundance of information down to a few key details for your players to digest. You don't overload them with concepts and strategies that compete for their attention and cause them to think too much during a game.

Preparing your team to play its best against a particular opponent takes time, ingenuity, and diligence. In this chapter we first cover the scouting and strategizing that's needed to develop a game plan. We then discuss the methods of communication and on-court preparation that best enables players to implement the game plan effectively.

DEVELOPING A GAME PLAN

As you have probably seen many times over, a well-prepared, overachieving team with an excellent game plan often has great success over a more skilled team that might be less focused and underprepared. Unless your squad is an Olympic dream team, it's way more effective to anticipate and react to what you know is coming than to try to improvise on the fly.

The first step in developing a game plan is gathering information about your opponent. A consistent method of gathering data and a template on which to record the information leads to a comprehensive scouting report. A consistent method also helps players form a habit of studying and assimilating information.

The second step is analyzing the data through the filter of your own team. For instance, say that after studying film you determine your next opponent can't handle full-court pressure. Does this mean you quickly draw up a new press for your players to learn and practice to prepare for the upcoming contest? Maybe, but just as likely not. Your decision depends on your players. If your players know nothing but a half-court defense, or if they lack the athleticism required to press, you're not going to want to risk changing your defense. The key to preparing for a game is planning to neutralize an opponent's strengths and exploiting their weaknesses with what your own team does well.

Scouting

The best way to obtain information about another team is to watch them play—either in person or via game footage on video. Each method has its advantages and disadvantages. When neither is possible, a coach should talk with another coach or source who's familiar with the opponent. Though not nearly as information-rich as the visual choices, verbal communication is far better than nothing, as long as the source is knowledgeable and trustworthy.

All members of a coaching staff should watch game film, but some staffs disperse the duties, assigning a lead scout for each team who's responsible for making sure the report is comprehensive and presenting the information to the head coach. When possible, the lead scout also gathers the opponent's roster and statistics. Game-by-game statistics of the contests on film provide a staff with a snapshot of those games, whereas cumulative season stats give a more accurate view of each player's contributions to the team.

Scouting Methods

A team's method of scouting depends largely on its level of competition, size of staff and budget, geography, availability of game footage, and governing regulations. An NCAA Division I basketball staff will dissect video of several of the opponent's games before taking the floor, but rules prohibit them from scouting in person except for games played in tournaments in which the team is participating. High schools located in close proximity to their opponents can send a representative to opposing teams' contests when scheduling conflicts prevent the coaches themselves from attending, but few have an abundance of game footage to watch.

A coach at any level can be best prepared for an opponent by using game film to reinforce in-person scouting. Whenever reasonable, an open exchange policy among teams—especially those with common opponents—will help more than hurt in the long run.

In Person High school coaches have a great advantage because they can scout in person. There are several benefits to taking in a game live. You can see the action on the court more clearly than on film. You can hear and see the verbal and nonverbal play calls. You can watch when, how, and who communicates the next play.

You can also factor in the environment and emotion surrounding the game action. How players react to various situations is invaluable information. Are they rattled or intimated by boisterous crowds? Are they flat in an empty gym? Do they lose focus when a call goes against them? Do they point fingers when a teammate makes a poor decision? How well do they fight back when momentum shifts to the other side? How effectively do they use time-outs and dead-ball situations?

Scouting in person is a combination of art and science and like any other skill it takes practice. The obvious disadvantages to watching a game live is the inability to pause, rewind, and fast-forward fast-paced action, and the inability to really study what both teams are doing on the same play. One way to avoid missing information is having multiple coaches scouting. The division of labor might be by teams, with each one taking down everything their assigned team is doing, or by side of the ball, with one focusing on all offensive play and the other all defensive play. If scouting alone, using a recorder and then transcribing the notes immediately after the game gives the coach another opportunity to process the action when it's still fresh.

On Video Although breaking down video might seem the easiest and most direct way to collect the most information about another team, it can quickly become overwhelming. How many games should you break down? How much time should players spend watching video instead of practicing on the court? Before either of these questions can be considered, a coach must have the equipment on which to watch and edit the video, an ability to use it, and the time to do so.

Generally speaking, studying three games usually provides a well-rounded feel for a team's players, various offenses, style of defense, favorite dead-ball plays, preferred game speed, and any trends or intangibles that inevitably surface for a keen eye. Watching game film of a team playing a common opponent helps put those performances in perspective.

A 32- or 40-minute game can be edited down to 12 to 15 minutes of valuable footage—plenty enough to show players the highlights of an opponent's offensive, defensive, and transitional style. Any more than that and some players will lose focus, as well as the court time practicing their own plays.

Anatomy of a Scouting Report

Scouting reports come in all shapes and sizes. Those that precede a big game or originate in a program with multiple staffers, a scouting budget, and access to statistics and game footage will of course be more elaborate than one-coach shops who are isolated geographically and digitally from their opponents. One size does not fit all, but the size that fits no one is a scouting report that confuses players by its complexity.

The sample scouting report at the end of this chapter (p. 9) tends toward the very complete. The report provides details on how players, individually, and the team, collectively, execute on the court, taking virtually all possible situations into account. This report also covers patterns of behavior, includes a detailed one-page summary of the finer points of play, and presents keys to winning the game, logistics of the trip or game day, and any out-of-the-ordinary aspects of the contest.

A scouting report includes video clips of opponents when available. When used in combination with game film, the order in which the game film is shown to players should correspond to the order in which the plays appear on the scouting report. For instance, if the video starts with a team running a cross-screen/back-screen action play, that should also be the first play on paper. This kind of organization saves time when reviewing the report and keeps the focus on the material.

Personnel It's best to give players their anticipated defensive assignment as soon as possible after the preceding game is over to prepare them for what they're going to face next. This starts with making sure they know their players' number and name. Attention is generally focused on players who will be on the court for at least 25 percent of the game.

Explain each player's value to her team: why she is on the floor and what she does well. As a rule, players will have one dominant move that they default to or rely on in pressure situations, whether it's pulling up at the three-point line, driving to the middle as soon as she touches the ball, or spinning off a defensive stop for a jump shot. But informing players of that move isn't enough. Teach them how to take that strength away and how to exploit the opponent's defensive and offensive weaknesses.

As a coaching staff, consider ways to create mismatches. If the opponent has a smaller guard, create situations to get the ball to your physical guard and give her the green light to drive or shoot. If the opponent switches defensively, prepare your team to play against the switch and, specifically, to set up further mismatches.

Keep stats about each opposing player as succinct as possible. A grid on the first page of the report should include the player's number, name, position, height, class, points per game, rebounds per game, field-goal percentage (with number of attempts and makes), three-point field-goal percentage (with number of attempts and makes), free-throw percentage (with number of attempts and makes), average minutes played per game, and total number of assists and turnovers.

Offensive Plays   Include the three to four most frequently used offensive sets each opponent uses against a man-to-man defense. Generally speaking, a team has either a primary offense or, if it's a quick hitter–oriented team that runs several different plays, an offense with fall-back plays to use in critical or quick-score situations. If you know the opponent's play call (i.e., a signal, hand gesture, or audible call), label the play as such so players can identify it quickly during the game. Otherwise, assign the play a descriptive name to use when you see the play developing. Then pick out two places within the offense to stop either their initiation process or the desired action. The same should be done with a team's top one or two offenses against the various zone defenses.

If it appears the opponent has never, or rarely, faced a zone defense, consider springing a zone on them for a couple of possessions out of dead-ball situations to see how their players react. In all cases, the idea is to identify tendencies and prepare to take away the specific shots the opponent most wants to take.

Transitions   Most teams have a primary fast break to get down the floor as quickly as possible, hoping to score several easy buckets during a game. Many teams also have a more controlled, structured secondary break for situations when the offensive and defensive numbers are the same. Identifying the times when the opponent employs the fast break (off makes, misses, or both), the primary ball handlers, and the players who force the tempo helps slow down their break and possibly create turnovers. If the opponent uses a long pass or outlet to half-court or beyond, plan to shadow the players that get down the floor early to ensure no offensive players get behind the deepest defender.

Special Situations   Special situations include out-of-bounds plays, last-second out-of-bounds plays, plays when the shot clock is running down, and late-game tendencies. For out-of-bounds plays, whether they originate under the basket or on the sidelines, first identify the player alignment. If the alignment changes for every play, it's easier to prepare your team for how to defend each play. If the alignment is the same for every play, determine whether certain player shifts in the formation tip a certain action, such as one player moving first for one play and another player moving first for another.

Knowing a team's favorite play or two during critical situations gives your team the advantage when the game is on the line. From where does the opponent like to initiate their specific action? Who do they want to have the basketball? Make them deviate from their plan, even if it's necessary to call a time-out to remind your team of their anticipated action and how to stop it.

Defense   Pick apart the opponent's defense. Do they have a poor defender who neglects to get into help defense, so that when the ball is on the opposite side of the court a player can drive to the basket knowing she only needs to beat her player? Do they have a poor on-ball defender who fouls often or can't contain off the dribble? How do they handle screens?

An opponent's press defense should also be evaluated. Where do they like to initiate the press—full court, three-quarter-court, or half-court? Is it a man-to-man, zone, or matchup zone press? When are they most likely to press? Do they trap out of the press, trying to create a turnover, or is their press used primarily to shave seconds off the shot clock? If they do trap, in which areas do they tend to trap, and which players are usually involved? What are their rotations on the floor, and who covers specific spots?

Keys to the Game Details are important, but too many muddle a mind. A coach's job is to take the details, synthesize them into the most important points, and then emphasize those points to the team during practice and games. Trying to do too much waters down the effectiveness of any one of the goals. Give players no more than two or three sentences on each facet of the game—offense, defense, and transition—that tells them how to win the contest.

Team Tendencies Coaches and teams tend to follow the same patterns, falling back on the same plays or players in tight games or coming out of dead-ball situations. Maybe they like to change things up defensively coming out of a time-out or when the ball is taken out on the side, or maybe they prefer to press at a certain time. If their team is down, they might rush shots or pull a quick trigger beyond the arc. Against a physical defense, a player might be more perimeter-oriented rather than playing in the post. Simply knowing that can help your players react to it more to your advantage, but sometimes a specific play or action can be scripted to counteract that tendency. Knowing what to expect at different times in a game is a major advantage.

Logistics and Setting Travel plans and the environment surrounding home and away games are important factors in preparing mentally and physically for a competition. It's amazing how much more at ease an entire travel party will be, families included, when they all have information about departure and arrival times, lodging details, and meal plans. Players can know they'll be fueled for the contest, and parents can arrange their trip with the team's itinerary in mind, abiding by any team policies regarding family time, of course.

Distractions are common elements in sports and can pop up unexpectedly. However, some distractions are predictable and can be negated with coaching. Will a sell-out crowd be on hand? If so, tell your team so they can steel themselves for the opposition and the noise. They'll also need to practice alternative methods of communication, such as hand signals and placards. Are you expecting a lifeless gymnasium? Coach your players to provide the energy and fill the place with their own enthusiasm. Is the home team introduced with a flamboyant production? Desensitize your team from the awe by talking about it. Will your team have to wait through a pregame ceremony, such as Senior Day, or extended media time-outs? If so, let your players know how to spend the time.

Detailed Checklist The last page of the scouting report provides a checklist of what to know about an opponent. Every important aspect of a team is covered, from player depth and how they use screens offensively to their ability to switch defensively and if they shoot threes in transition—and everything in between. The checklist paints a vivid picture of the opposing team so that your team can begin considering how to alter that picture to its benefit.

Strategizing

Once the scouting report is complete, you want to distill the information into a plan that gives your team the best chance of winning. As we mentioned earlier, the plan starts with your own team and knowing its strengths. Who's the best defensive player? Who's the worst? Who's the best defensive perimeter player? Who's the best defensive post player? Who are the best rebounders?

Only after these determinations have been made should the opponent factor into your plan. Who are their best players? What players must they have on the floor to win the game? Who are their best rebounders? Your plan unfolds as a way to nullify strengths and exploit weaknesses. Unless your best player is overwhelmingly your best defensive player, having her guard their best player isn't always the best option because it sets her up for foul trouble. A better plan is to identify their biggest threat on the perimeter and assign her to your defensive stopper, and do the same thing in the post. Then develop a two-deep depth chart of who will potentially guard each person on the opposing team projected to play at least 25 percent of the game.

A team might have 20 offensive looks, but chances are they won't execute all of them well. As you study the scouting report, a team's bread and butter should become apparent. It might be their post play or that their guards dominate their games. They might draw fouls and get to the line more than usual; they might have sharp shooters from three-point range; they might be an excellent rebounding team; they might play smothering defense. Identify the plays, the offensives, the cuts—whatever is essential to their team. If a team seems to lack a clear identity, break things down statistically, charting how many times they run each play.

Of course, a team might do more than one thing very well, but be careful about building up a team to sound unbeatable by emphasizing all of the areas in which they're great. Instead, focus on neutralizing what they consider their biggest advantage, or at least the advantage you believe your team can best influence. Negating that strength might throw off a team enough to shake their confidence or disrupt their timing.

IMPLEMENTING A GAME PLAN

No matter how brilliant or carefully crafted, a game plan is not worth the paper it's written on if players can't execute it. Remember that games are won on the court, not on paper or in a film room. Thus it's critical that players understand the concepts of the game plan and can perform the skills required to carry it out.

The culmination of the scouting and scheming is game day. Can your team put your plan into action when it counts? Can you read the flow of the game and draw up just the right play at just the right time to give your team a quick emotional lift, a key stop, or a game-winning bucket?

Preparation

Preparation for an opponent occurs in up to three phases: the written scouting report, film sessions (when available), and the on-court practice that puts theory into action. Each phase builds on the previous: players read the critical information on the opponent, see the concepts on game film, and make the concepts come to life on the court.

The standard lead time before facing an opponent is two to four days, except during tournament play and interruptions in the schedule for final exams or holidays. Developing a routine of when players receive the written report, watch film sessions, and hit the court will maximize not only the time to prepare but also your players' ability to shift focus from one game to the next.

Off-Court

Coaches need to be at least a game ahead in terms of scouting so that the written report and the video report (when available) for the next opponent are ready immediately after the preceding game, or else two to three days in advance of the contest—whichever comes first.

One method of introducing material to the team is distributing the written report at the beginning of the film session for that opponent, which the lead coach for that opponent will have prepared. After an explanation of the one aspect of the game the opponent relies on, the lead coach reviews the personnel in the order listed on the report, always starting with the point guard and moving through the other players, and always talking directly to the players who will be guarding those players.

The video session should highlight the offensive plays the opponent employs most often, with four being the maximum. Including every look an opponent has will overload your players and dilute the impact that presenting the key plays has on them. Start with offense before moving to the fast-break and secondary-break systems, out-of-bounds plays under the basket, sideline out-of-bounds plays, defensive schemes or style, man-to-man defenses, zone defenses, and presses. Include not only clips of the opponent executing well but also clips in which another team has disrupted that play, showing your players the cracks in the opponent's armor. Arrange the clips so that they appear in descending order of the frequency with which they are used and in the same order as they are drawn on the written report. In some cases, players might want their own copy of the video clip to study on their own.

On-Court

To emphasize in theory and in practice that focusing on your own team is more important than focusing on an opponent, limit the time on scouting report sessions to no more than 15 to 20 minutes per day. After that, your players will start to lose interest and focus. First, explain the play and have players or the scout team walk through it. Then demonstrate specific ways to stop that specific action.

Be organized and move efficiently through the material, walking through their offenses and special plays and explaining what they'll do against a press defense. The last thing you want to do is lecture for an hour. Move fast enough to get players thinking; replicate gamelike situations as much as possible.

One way to maximize retention is to cover the written scouting report, watch film, hit the floor, and after practice cover the written report and film session again. This way, players read it, hear it, see it, physically experience it, and then hear it and see it again to tie it all together. After two or three days of this routine, they should be well-versed on the other team's identity.

Game Day

Game-day preparation will vary among individuals. Every player should have the relative freedom to gear up for a game in the way that works best for her. But basketball is a team sport, and at some point the team must come together and prepare as a unit. The timing might vary depending on competition level and logistics, but including the following points and keeping the routine consistent are what matter most.

Have your team meet in the locker room about an hour before tipoff to review the main bullet points of the opponent's personnel, offense, and defense; the team's offense and defense; and three keys to be effective and win the game. This meeting should not be a learning session, nor is it the forum for presenting new information unless it concerns an injury, officials, or game atmosphere. Your intent is to get players thinking specifically about the game and their assignments.

Sample Written Scouting Report
Team Us vs. Team Them

Team Them Personnel

Starters	Position	Height	Cl	Points	Rebounds	Field Goal %	3FG %	Free Throw %	Minutes Played	Matchup
#4 Jane Doe	1	5'7"	SR	6	2	38% 43–112	38% 23–61	64% 18–28	24	
Aggressive PG who controls her tempo and runs her team very well. Keeps them organized in the half-court and pushes the ball hard in the full court. Constantly looking to get the ball inside to #24 and #21. Will shoot the 3 when left open and drive (RH) vs. pressure when there's no pass to be made. No transition—stop the ball! Pressure.										61 Assists 41 TOs
#31 Susie Doe	2	5'7"	SR	9	2	40% 63-156	37% 47-126	70% 14-20	28	
3-point shooter! Is a catch-and-shoot player who loves to put it up. Most of her attempts come from transition and/or kickouts from post drives and kicks from #5. Looks to go off ball screens/handoffs to shoot the 3. Must know where she is. No free looks!										34 Assists 22 TOs
#5 Sarah Doe	2/3	5'7"	SO	11	3	41% 67-165	29% 13-45	84% 61-73	27	
Scoring wing and best overall player. Very aggressive with and without the ball. Constantly looking to get the ball in her hands. Favorite move is to catch, shot fake, then drive. Will drive until she's stopped or puts it off the glass. She will shoot the 3, but only if she doesn't have a driving lane or is wide open. Loves to drive to the middle of the floor for a pull-up J or pass down low to #21 and #24. No middle! Pressure and contain.										52 Assists 61 TOs
#21 Sally Doe	4	6'1"	JR	9	7	53% 79-150	0% 0-1	84% 42-49	31	
Athletic post player who does a very good job of screening and rebounding. She likes to set ball screens on the perimeter and roll to low block. Will duck in hard when she is weakside looking for an angle to the basket. Turnaround J in the post. We must box her out and keep her off the boards. No second-chance points. No free angles. Box!										45 Assists 51 TOs
#24 Ashley Doe	4	5'11"	JR	9	6	57% 81-143	0% 0-0	57% 34-60	26	
Most active post player and the player they look for the most in their offense. Plays down low and is very good at using her body for seals and duck-ins. Finishes with either hand in the post. Favorite move is a fade-away over right shoulder. Has 15- to 17-ft range to hit the high post J. We must have our feet above hers to take away the weak-side duck-in. Active rebounder who gets her hands on a lot of balls. Box out!										17 Assists 43 TOs
Subs										
#40 Amanda Doe	3/4	5'11"	SO	7	3	37% 43-117	20% 6-30	80% 24-30	20	
Physical wing/post player who gets a lot of points in the paint. Stocky and likes to use her body to post smaller guards. Slips screens to post. Drives (RH) when pressured. Contain.										35 Assists 48 TOs
#33 Amy Doe	3/4	5'10"	SR	5	2	53% 38-71	60% 6-10	62% 23-37	16	
Athletic wing/post player who screens and defends very well. Will fake shot and drive when pressured. Not a primary threat but has the ability to go off at any time. Pressure.										19 Assists 41 TOs
#54 Liza Doe	5	6'1"	SR	5	3	59% 42-71	0% 0-0	69% 9-13	13	
Big physical post player who is their only true 5. Posts hard toward the ball, looking for lobs/angles to the basket. 10- to 15-ft range. Keep her off the boards—no seals or duck-ins.										8 Assists 34 TOs
#12 Jenny Doe	1	5'9"	FR	5	2	35% 28-79	31% 12-39	87% 14-16	19	
Backup PG who is aggressive with the ball and tempo. Pushes the ball hard in transition, looking to throw over the top for easy points. Shot fake drive in the half court. Pressure.										27 Assists 40 TOs

Sample Written Scouting Report

TEAM THEM OFFENSE

- 4 Out/1 In with duck-ins by #24 and #21. High ball screens/wing ball screens
- Box sets to free up #31 and #5 to get the ball in scoring position
- High/low game in transition

Sample Written Scouting Report

TEAM THEM DEFENSE

- They are primarily a man-to-man, half-court team that likes to pressure the ball and put the other four players in the paint. They will let you run your offense but will play passing lanes a step outside the three-point line. Their ball pressure tries to force the dribble and take away the pass.

- On all ball screens they like to go underneath the screen. The post player will show, and the guard will go all the way underneath and then rotate back to the ball.

- Baseline out-of-bounds defense is man to man with inbounds defender facing the action/taking first cut.

- They have used a 2-3 zone and a 2-3 trap in the majority of the games they have played. In the 2-3 regular they use the back line to cover wings before the top guards can recover.

- The 2-3 trap is easy to see coming. They extend it out close to half-court. They'll trap on top after you cross the center line and trap on the wings.

- They have shown a 1-2-2 three-quarter court press but rarely use it.

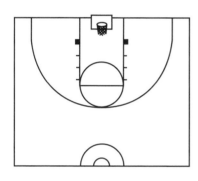 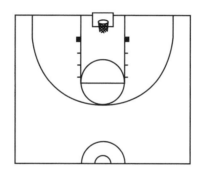 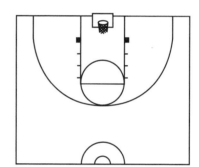

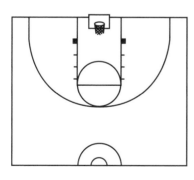 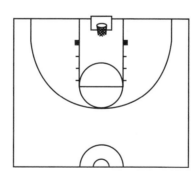 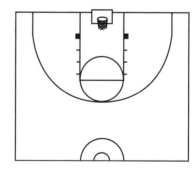

Sample Written Scouting Report

TEAM THEM OUT OF BOUNDS

- All OBs are out of a different alignment.
- They look for free layups and three-point shots.

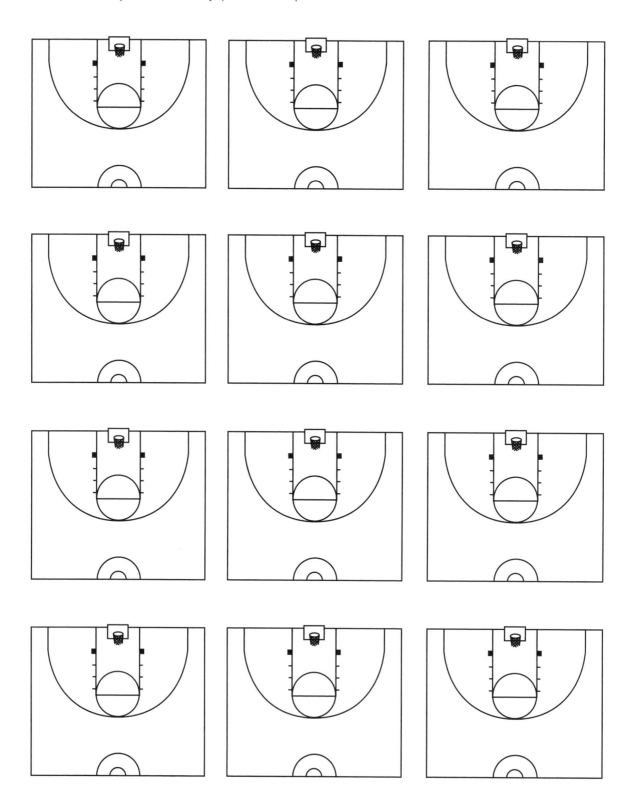

Sample Written Scouting Report

TEAM THEM PRESS OFFENSE

Vs. 2-2-1

Vs. Contain

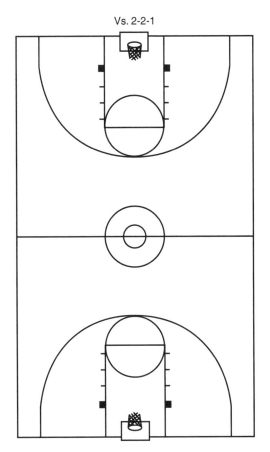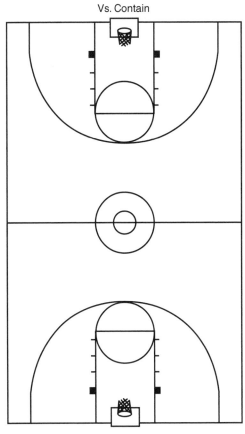

DEFENSIVE KEYS TO THE GAME

- BALL PRESSURE. They are active on offense and really like to get the ball inside, either on a post entry or on drives to the basket. We **must** apply good ball pressure and keep the ball sideline while forcing it baseline.

- HELP and RECOVER. They *love* to penetrate vs. *pressure. All of them will catch / fake-shot / drive.* On any reversal or quick pass they all look to drive to the basket. Be in help-side and rotate over to take a *CHARGE!!!* They drive to score first, pass second. A very physical team that doesn't mind contact in the lane. Be sure to stop *all* penetration outside the paint!

- BALL SCREEN DEFENSE. The biggest and most consistent part of their offense is the ball screen. They like to screen on the wing and set a high screen at the top of the key. Their first look is for the opposite post player ducking in hard. Their second look is the kickback to the screener. Their third look is to take the ball to the basket for points and fouls. We must communicate and play smart.

- REBOUND. Box them out! They are very good at tapping the ball out to get another possession. They don't get a lot of clean rebounds, but they're scrappy and try to create a lot of loose balls to run down. We must *pull through* the ball and secure it at every opportunity.

- TRANSITION D. They push the ball on makes and misses. #4 and #5 are very active in their transition game. They like to push hard, and #24 and #21 will fill the lane to the basket. #31 really likes to spot up in transition for free looks. STOP THE BALL quick!!!

Sample Written Scouting Report

OFFENSIVE KEYS TO THE GAME

- EXECUTE. Make every possession count. Good decisions and high-percentage basketball.
- RELOCATE / STAY AVAILABLE. They like to play behind the post. Get help from opposite post.
- ATTACK. They will let us run our offense. Take what we want!
- FUNDAMENTAL. Be ready to play against pressure. Execute and stick to the fundamentals. Make them guard good screens and cuts! Consistent with *our* game!

GENERAL	Yes	No	Notes
Deep bench?			
Strong inside game?			
Strong perimeter game?			
Good foul shooting team?			
Good rebounding team?			
Good transition team?			
Good defensive fundamentals			
TEAM OFFENSE	**Yes**	**No**	**Notes**
Set play offense?			
Motion offense?			
Fast-break system?			
Do they use screens? What type?			
Do they initiate their offense a specific way?			
Do they have good passing skills?			
Do they use the shot clock effectively?			
Do they have a specific offensive strength?			
Do they have a specific offensive weakness?			
Do all perimeter players handle the ball?			
Do they have more than one effective post?			
Do they exhibit a specific type of post play?			
Do they use a lot of backdoors?			
Do they use post splits or handoffs?			
Do they rely on a system or athleticism?			
TEAM DEFENSE	**Yes**	**No**	**Notes**
Do they play multiple defenses?			
Do they press full court?			
Do they trap full, three-quarter, or half court?			

Sample Written Scouting Report

TEAM DEFENSE (continued)	Yes	No	Notes
Do they utilize defensive stunts? What type?			
Do they play junk defenses?			
Are they capable of pressuring the ball?			
Are they fundamentally sound with footwork?			
Do they help and recover well?			
Do they effectively defend the post?			
Do they switch?			
Where can they exert the greatest pressure?			
Do they have a specific defensive strength?			
Do they have specific weaknesses?			

TRANSITION	Yes	No	Notes
Do they effectively use the break? Type?			
Secondary break?			
Do they shoot threes in transition?			
Are they effective at inbounding and outletting the ball?			
Are they effective in defensive transition? How?			
Do they pressure the outlet or rebounder?			
Are their big players effective at getting back?			

CHAPTER

2

Fast-Break Offense

Most coaches have a love-hate relationship with the fast break. When run well—players hustling downcourt, great ballhandling, crisp passing, sharing the ball, finishing the shot—the fast break can invigorate a team, deflate an opponent, attract and thrill a crowd, seal a game, and make a coach look brilliant. When executed poorly—lethargic players, poor decisions, multiple turnovers, missed opportunities—the fast break can cause teams to tank, spectators to groan, and coaches' hair to turn gray.

The most opportunistic scenario for a fast break is when the ball changes possession quickly and the offense gets more players up the floor than the defense: one defender is forced to guard two players, two defenders must guard three, etc. A fast break can be successful when the offensive players equal those on defense, but it is highly discouraged when the defenders outnumber the attackers.

A fast break can materialize on many occasions—after a steal, turnover, missed shot, or made shot—and with players at any spot on the floor. This means each player should know how to fill each position on the court. The keys to an effective fast break are to take care of the basketball, spread the floor, and find that balance of pushing the tempo in a controlled manner when you have a numbers advantage over the opponent. The speed of two or more players, at least relative to the opponent, is a contributing factor in creating fast-break chances, but it doesn't automatically mean they will result in a score.

In the purest sense, a fast break isn't really a play at all, although there are ways to confound the opponent with cuts, screens, and passes that can open up an otherwise deadlocked situation. As the name implies, the fast break is rapid in developing and can create an uncomplicated opportunity to score an easy basket. To initiate the break, you get the ball to a ball handler. The nearest players, or those who can do so most quickly, fill the lanes and stay aware at all times. The ball handler looks to pass first and dribble second. Either way, the ball is moved rapidly upcourt for an easy shot. Trailers hustle downcourt for the rebound.

A fast-break opportunity doesn't have to end if that first shot isn't available or if it doesn't fall, which is when most of the plays in this chapter come in handy. Whereas most teams transition from a missed fast-break opportunity into a set offense, well-coached teams transition from a primary break into a secondary break. Doing so often presents yet another open, easy look at the basket because it catches the opponent in a lull, attacking when the defense is relaxed between disrupting the fast break and establishing its bearings to play half-court formation.

Secondary breaks can take a number of forms and lead to a variety of opportunities, such as setting screens for trailers, taking advantage of a size mismatch either inside or on the perimeter with defenders out of position, and giving a long-range shooter time to set for an open look behind the three-point arc.

As is true for fast breaks, secondary plays don't always lead to a score, and the temptation to force the action instead of letting a play develop or knowing when to transition into a half-court offensive set can sometimes lead to turnovers. However, the unrelenting pressure that primary and secondary breaks puts on an opponent outweighs the occasional mistake.

2 CLEAR OUT

Charli Turner Thorne

Objectives

- To kick the ball up early and put pressure on the opponent to defend the perimeter shot.
- To clear out the low post and give a perimeter player space to create her shot.

When to Use

- When a defender does not move her feet.
- When an opponent lacks great help-side defense.

Key Personnel

Your 2 player must be able to set up her penetration with a fake and quick first step. She must be able to hit a jump shot or keep her dribble if the defense recovers. The 3 player must be able to cut into the paint and shoot a midrange shot off the catch.

Execution

1. 1 passes to 2 on the wing. 4 steps out to set a fake on-ball screen (figure 1).
2. 2 penetrates to the basket as 3 flashes into the lane and 5 drops with the ball (figure 2).

Points of Emphasis

The defense might aggressively deny 1's kick-up pass to 2, who will have to work hard to get open on her own with proper timing, speed, and change of direction. The 2 must do a great job setting up her defense, pretending to use the ball screen, before she penetrates. The 4 can help by talking ("Use my screen!") while setting the fake screen. As the defense drops to the line of the ball and executes aggressive help-side defense, the 2 finds the open player on the weak side. The 3 must time her cut into the lane well, because she risks bringing her defender to the ball if she cuts too soon.

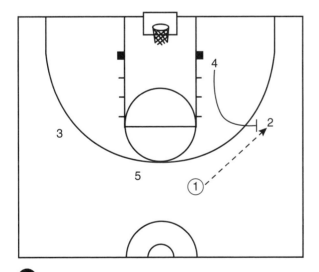

1

2

3 GAP

Charli Turner Thorne

Objectives

- To kick the ball up early and pressure the opponent to defend the perimeter shot or ball-side post feed.
- To create a midrange shot in the paint for a perimeter player.

When to Use

When the defense has done a good job of picking up man to man in transition because the floor is spaced well and the ball-side defenders are occupied.

Key Personnel

Your 3 player must be able to set up her defense, cut hard, and read how the defense is playing her. She must be able to catch the ball on the move and hit a jump shot from 10 to 15 feet (3-4.5 m). Your 4 must take pride in getting her teammate open by setting a good screen.

Execution

1 passes to 2. 4 sets a lateral screen for 3, who cuts into the gap and pulls up for the jumper (figure 1).

Variation

The defense might deny 1's kick-up pass to 2. If this happens, 1 dribbles to the wing while 2 cuts through to the weak-side baseline. The play continues with 4 setting the cross-screen for 3. The 1 player passes to 3 (figure 2).

Points of Emphasis

This play is best run to a shooter who is able to catch and shoot on the move. On the catch, 2 quickly looks to see if 5 is open for a quick pass and shot. Otherwise, 2 occupies her defender in a triple-threat position while waiting for 4 to screen for 3, whose cut must be well timed, and give herself enough space to get the shot off. If 3 is a left-handed shooter, the play is best run in mirror image, with 3 coming from the right to the middle.

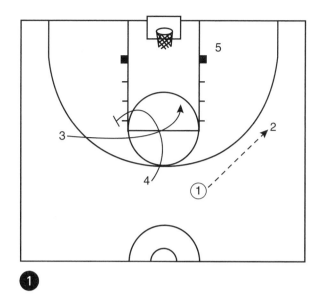

1

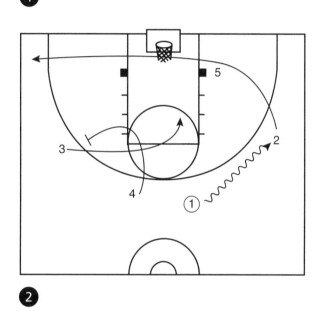

2

FLAT-ON BALL

Charli Turner Thorne

Objectives

- To space the floor and assist the point guard in relieving pressure.
- To occupy the weak side during a three-on-three situation.

When to Use

Any time against a man-to-man defense.

Key Personnel

The 1 player must be able to read the defense and create offense off the dribble. The 2 must be able to hit the perimeter shot. The 4 should be able to catch the ball on the move.

Execution

1. 4 leaves the low block and sets an on-ball screen at the right elbow for 1, who goes right or left off the screen. 5 sets a down screen for 3 (figure 1).
2. 4 rolls to the basket and 2 drops immediately.
3. 1 passes to either 4 or 2 (figure 2).

Variation

If 5's defender is sitting in the paint, 1 might not be able to pass to 4 rolling to the basket. The 1 player then looks for 3 coming off 5's screen (figure 3).

Points of Emphasis

The point guard must push the ball upcourt and attack before the defense is set. The angle of 4's screen—it should be flat and low—is a determining factor in creating an open shot for the guard or the switch that leads to a mismatch. This screen should be set with 4's back to the basket. The screen puts pressure on the post defender to make a quick decision, and a switch causes a mismatch that results in a guard defending a post inside the paint. Typically, 5 will be trailing the play after grabbing the rebound. If the ball has been pushed up the floor, 5 will head right into screening for 3.

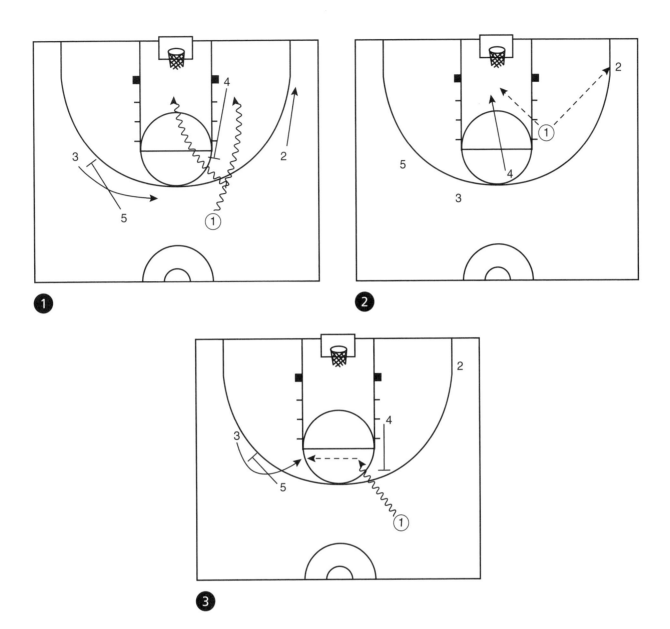

SKIP AND SEAL

Charli Turner Thorne

Objectives

- To get a perimeter shooter open and to change the angle for a post feed.
- To take advantage of a defense clogging up the middle or overhelping in the paint.

When to Use

When facing a defense that fronts or aggressively denies the pass into the post.

Key Personnel

Your 2 player must be an accurate skip-passer. Your 3 must have good range. Your 5 understands how to set up her defense and seal on the pass.

Execution

1. 1 passes to 2. 4 screens 3's defender so 3 can pop out to the wing and receive the skip pass from 2 (figure 1).
2. 5 seals her player on the weak side or flashes across the lane for a post feed. 3 either shoots or feeds 5 as 4 clears to the top of the key (figure 2).

Variations

- There are times when 4's defense is clogging the middle, or when 4 is a better finisher in the paint than 5 is. In this case, 4 dives to the basket after setting a screen for 3. The 4 finds her defender and seals her in the paint. The 5 empties the low post by flash-cutting above the free-throw line. The 3 can pass to 4 on the low block or to 5 in the high post (figure 3).
- If 1 is unable to pass to 2, she dribbles to the wing and pushes 2 down. The 1 then makes the skip pass to 3 (figure 4).

Points of Emphasis

The 1 must keep her head up and kick the ball up to 2. The 3 spaces the floor high and wide and positions herself to be ready to catch and shoot. The 5 prepares her defense by pushing her higher or lower and is ready to seal on the skip pass. If 3 doesn't shoot the ball, she needs to be able to set the defense up to make the post feed.

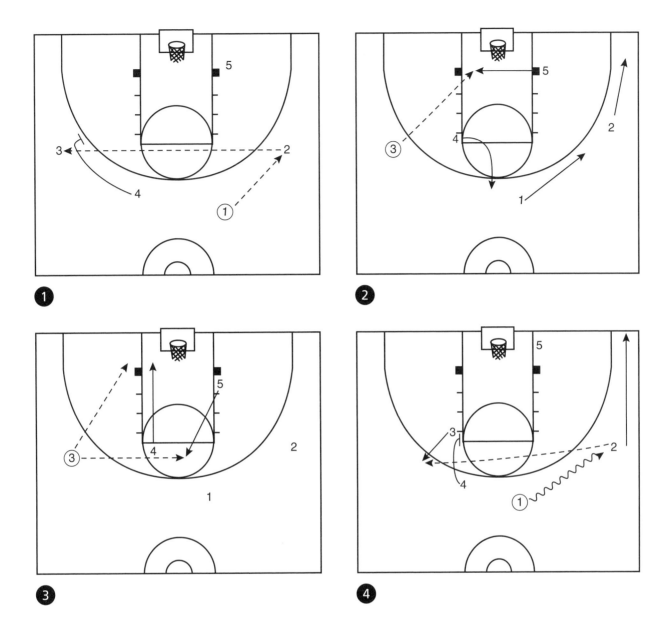

TRIPLE FLARE

Charli Turner Thorne

Objective

To clear out an area for penetration, screen for a shooter, or pass to a post player cutting to the basket.

When to Use

- When the defense has done a good job picking up man to man in transition.
- To get your point guard an early shot off a triple screen.

Key Personnel

Your 2 guard must be able to make the right read with the ball in her hands. Your 1 should be a good three-point shooter. Your 4 must have good timing in her cut to the basket.

Execution

1. 1 passes to 2. 5 cuts to the weak side, immediately opening a free lane that might allow 2 to drive to the basket (figure 1).
2. If not, 2 dribbles up as 4, 3, and 5 set a triple flare for 1, who receives the ball from 2 and shoots (figure 2).

Variation

When 4 is quicker than her defender or scores well cutting to the basket, or if she has a size advantage and can post up on the low block, a continuation of the play works well. The 4 slips to the basket after screening for 1. The 3 then fills the opposite wing as 5 flashes into the high post. The 2 passes to 4, 3, or 5. If 5 gets the ball, she has a high-post clear-out or can pass to 4 in the low post (figure 3).

Points of Emphasis

The 2 player must understand her options. The 4 must have good timing in her cut to the basket. If she cuts too early, 2 might not be able to get her the ball. The 1 should start her cut while watching 4, waiting if 4 cuts to the basket to cut off the double flare. In that case, 2 should be able to dribble toward 3 and make a shorter pass.

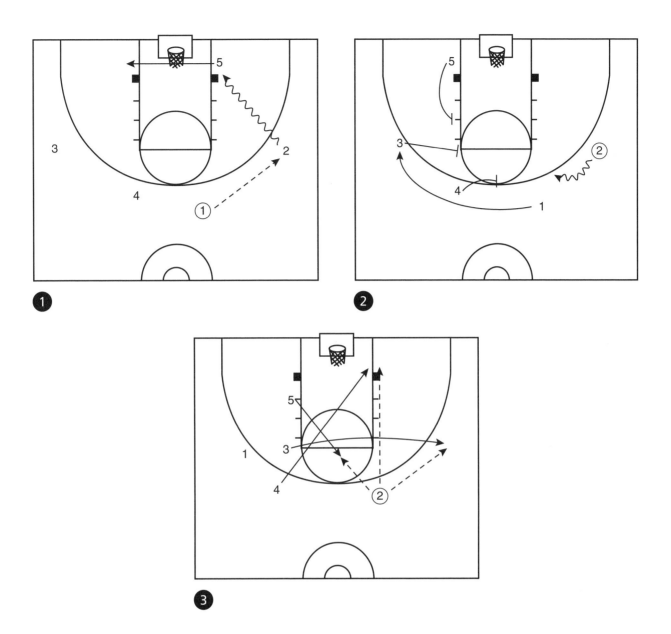

KANSAS

Tom Collen

Objective

To give players structure, with options to attack an opponent's defensive adjustments without slowing or stopping the flow of the game.

When to Use

- As a secondary offense when a team doesn't have the numbers advantage in transition.
- As a called play or an entrance into another offense.
- Against a man-to-man defense.

Key Personnel

Your 1 player must be a good ball handler and decision maker, an accurate passer, and able to make early reads about the type and weakness of the defense. Your 2 should be your best screener and an accurate three-point shooter. Your 3 is your most versatile guard, able to shoot from the perimeter, read post defenders, attack off the dribble, post up smaller defenders, and hit the offensive boards. Your 4 is your biggest guard or a power forward with versatility much like 3's. Your 5 is your best back-to-the-basket player; she has good hands and can score one on one or pass out of a double team.

Execution

1. In transition, 2 fills the right lane, 3 fills the left lane, and the first post, in this case 5, fills the middle. 1 pushes the ball on the dribble and passes it ahead to 2 only if 2 is set and ready to score (figure 1).

2. If neither 2 nor 5 is open, 1 reverses the ball to 4. 5 follows the ball, continuing to look for a post entry pass, and 2 moves in from dead corner to short corner (figure 2).

3. As the ball is reversed from 4 to 3, 5 continues to work for a pass. 2 sets a back screen for 4, who cuts off for a lob from 3. 1 moves to the free-throw line extended area (figure 3).

4. If 2's defender helps on 4, 2 steps out for a three-point shot (figure 4).

5. If 2 doesn't shoot, 5 sprints to set a high-ball screen and 4 replaces 5 (figure 5).

Points of Emphasis

Floor spacing is critical for preventing a defender from guarding two players at once. Your 1's ability to avoid the tempting pass up the floor to 2 unless 2 is clearly open and ready prevents costly turnovers and keeps the ball in the hands of your best decision maker. Crisp, quick ball movement based on what the defense is allowing usually results in open looks.

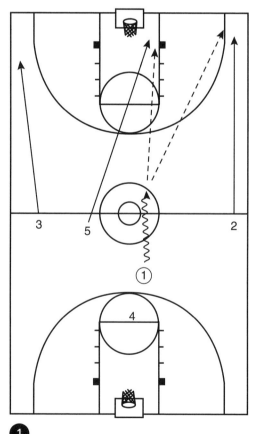

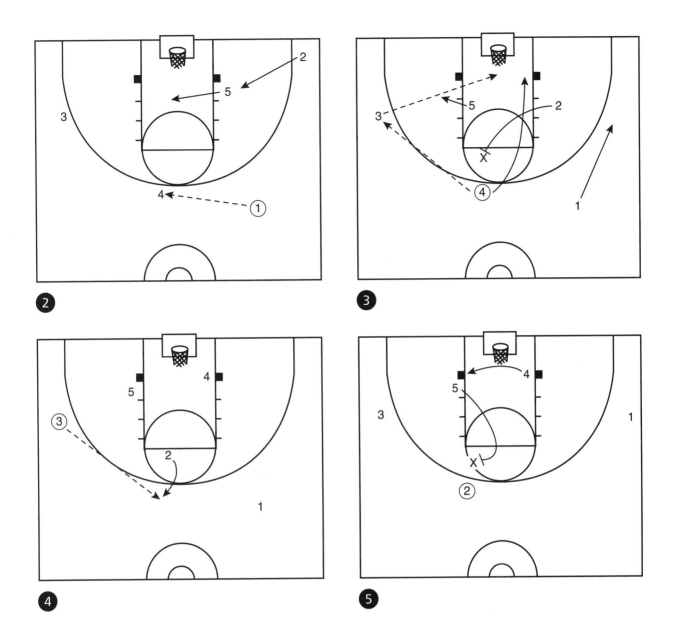

KANSAS FOUR

Tom Collen

Objective

To get the ball to the low-post player, a lob to an open post, or a pass to the point guard for a three-pointer.

When to Use

- As a secondary offense when a team doesn't have numbers in transition.
- As a called play or an entrance into another offense.
- When the trail post is being denied.
- Against a man-to-man defense.

Key Personnel

Your 1 player is a good ball handler, decision maker, and accurate passer and can make early reads on the type and weakness of the defense. Your 2 is your best screener and an accurate three-point shooter. Your 3 is your most versatile guard, able to shoot from the perimeter, read post defenders, attack off the dribble, post up smaller defenders, and hit the offensive boards. Your 4 is your biggest guard or a power forward with versatility much like 3's. Your 5 is your best back-to-the-basket player; she has good hands and can score one on one or pass out of a double team.

Execution

1. In transition, 2 fills the right lane, 3 fills the left lane, and the first post, in this case 5, fills the middle. 1 pushes the ball on the dribble and passes it ahead to 2 only if 2 is set and ready to score (see *Kansas*, figure 1, p. 28).

2. If 4's defender is preventing the pass to her, 4 sets a screen for 1, who drives past. 2 sprints to set a back screen on 4's defender. 5 follows the ball (figure 1).

3. 4 cuts off 2's screen looking for a lob pass. If 1's defender gets lost on the screen and 4's defender doesn't help, 1 will be open for a three-point shot, pull-up jumper, or easy post-entry pass to 5 (figure 2).

Variation

The 4 can pop out for a three-point shot if her defender tries to go low or under 2's screen.

Points of Emphasis

The 2 needs to set the screen as 1 brushes off 4. The 5 follows the ball, looking for a post-entry pass because this is now a one-on-one matchup with only 2's defender available to help. If the defenders guarding 2 and 4 switch on the back screen, 1 capitalizes on the mismatch and gets the ball inside to 4.

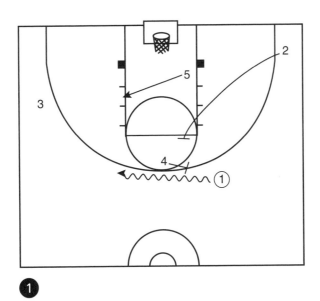

1

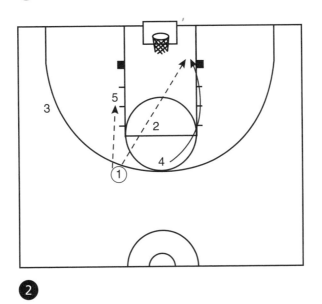

2

KANSAS SLIP

Tom Collen

Objective

To get the posts into a high-low game.

When to Use

- As a secondary offense when a team doesn't have numbers in transition.
- As a called play or an entrance into another offense.
- When the trailing post is being denied or if she can score on her defender one on one.
- Against a man-to-man defense.

Key Personnel

Your 1 must be a good ball handler and decision maker, an accurate passer, and able to make early reads on the type and weakness of the defense. Your 2 is your best screener and an accurate three-point shooter. Your 3 is your most versatile guard, able to shoot from the perimeter, read post defenders, attack off the dribble, post up smaller defenders, and hit the offensive boards. Your 4 is your biggest guard or a power forward with versatility much like 3's. Your 5 is your best back-to-the-basket player; she has good hands and can score one on one or pass out of a double team.

Execution

1. In transition, 2 fills the right lane, 3 fills the left lane, and 4 fills the middle. 1 pushes the ball on the dribble and passes it ahead to 2 only if 2 is set and ready to score. 5 trails (similar to figure 1 in *Kansas*, p. 28, but with 4 as the lead post).

2. 1 drives at 5 and her defender near the top of the circle. 5 then makes a backdoor cut to the basket. 4 sprints straight up the lane line to the three-point line, staying within shooting range (figure 1).

3. If 4's defender drops to prevent the backdoor pass, 1 quickly reverses the ball to 4, who has the option of passing to 5, shooting an open three-pointer, or driving to the basket as her defender rushes to recover (figure 2).

Variation

The 4 starts on the opposite post and runs outside the three-point line as 1 drives at 5. If 4's defender stays in to help on 5's slip or roll down, then 1 can pass to 4 for an open three or another high-low look (figure 3).

Points of Emphasis

The 4 must be aware of 2's defender rotating to help or to steal the pass from 1 to 4. If the defender makes this adjustment, one more pass to 2 in the corner will get your best three-point shooter an open shot.

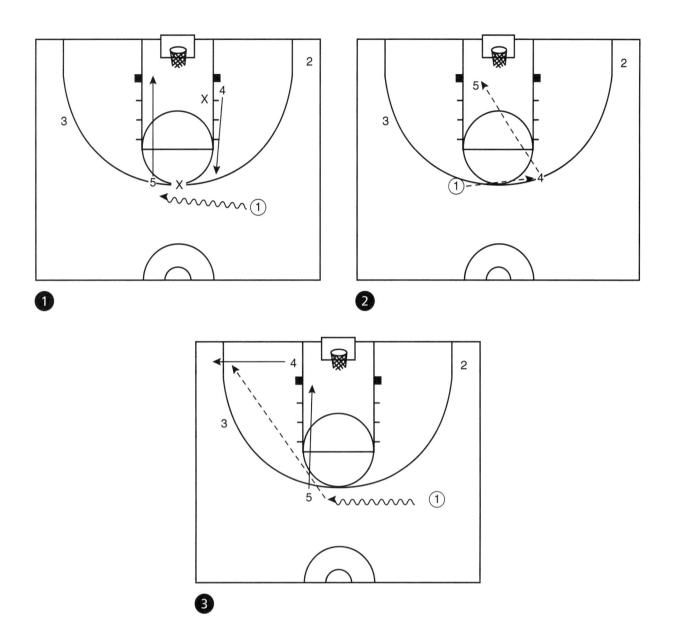

KANSAS THROWBACK

Tom Collen

Objective

To get the trail post a layup.

When to Use

- As a secondary offense when a team doesn't have numbers in transition.
- As a called play or an entrance into another offense.
- When 4 or 5 is the trail post and the defense is expecting the ball to be reversed, as in Kansas.
- Against a man-to-man defense.

Key Personnel

Your 1 player must be a good ball handler and decision maker, an accurate passer, and able to make early reads on the type and weakness of the defense. Your 2 is your best screener and an accurate three-point shooter. Your 3 is your most versatile guard, able to shoot from the perimeter, read post defenders, attack off the dribble, post up smaller defenders, and hit the offensive boards. Your 4 is your biggest guard or a power forward with versatility much like 3's. Your 5 is your best back-to-the-basket player; she has good hands and can score one on one or pass out of a double team.

Execution

1. In transition, 2 fills the right lane, 3 fills the left lane, and the first post, in this case 5, fills the middle. 1 pushes the ball on the dribble and passes it ahead to 2 only if 2 is set and ready to score (see *Kansas,* figure 1, p. 28).
2. If neither 2 nor 5 is open, 1 reverses the ball to 4. 5 follows the ball, continuing to look for a post-entry pass, and 2 moves in from dead corner to short corner (see *Kansas*, figure 2, p. 29)
3. If a defender is denying the pass from 4 to 3, 4 throws the ball back to 1, who has moved lower on the right wing. 2 continues to set a screen for 4, who cuts off the screen immediately following the pass to 1 (figure 1).
4. 1 looks for 4 cutting to the basket or 2 stepping out for a three-point shot (figure 2).

Variation

If 1 is being denied the throwback, 4 can use 2's screen like a ball screen and drive to the basket.

Points of Emphasis

The timing and angle of the screen are important. To avoid an illegal screen violation and to ensure the cutter gets open, the screen should be set as the ball is leaving 4's hands or as 4 drives to the basket.

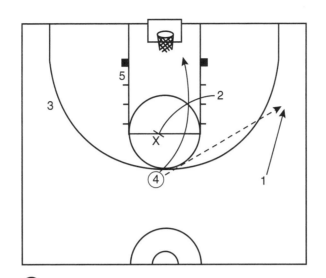

1

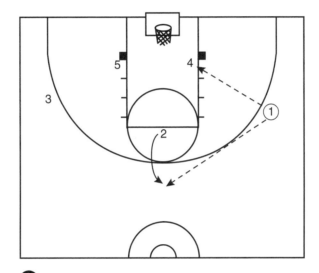

2

KANSAS ZONE

Tom Collen

Objective

To quickly attack a zone defense with the same secondary offense.

When to Use

When a defense is switching from man-to-man to zone defense to counter the secondary offense.

Key Personnel

Your 1 player must be a good ball handler and decision maker, an accurate passer, and able to make early reads on the type and weakness of the defense. Your 2 is your best screener and an accurate three-point shooter. Your 3 is your most versatile guard, able to shoot from the perimeter, read post defenders, attack off the dribble, post up smaller defenders, and hit the offensive boards. Your 4 is your biggest guard or a power forward with versatility much like 3's. Your 5 is your best back-to-the-basket player; she has good hands and can score one on one or pass out of a double team. Your 4 and 5 players must be able to make safe interior passes.

Execution

1. In transition, 2 fills the right lane, 3 fills the left lane, and 4 fills the middle. 1 pushes the ball on the dribble and passes it ahead to 2 only if 2 is set and ready to score. 5 trails (similar to figure 1 in *Kansas*, p. 28, but with 4 as the lead post).
2. If 1 can't make an early post-entry pass to 5, she passes to 4, who passes to 3 as 5 moves through the lane and to the short corner area (figure 1).
3. 4 dives into the gap in the zone. 2 sprints to the top of the key. 1 drops to the free-throw line extended area. 3 looks to 4 in the middle of the lane (figure 2).
4. If 4 isn't open, 3 looks to 5 in the short corner, who has the option of shooting, driving, hitting 4 in the middle, or passing to 1 or 2 (figure 3).
5. If 5 isn't open, 3 skips the ball to 1 or passes to 2 to enter into a zone offense.

Variation

The 3 dribbles to the top of the key as 4 is flaring to the opposite wing for a three-point shot. The 1 and 2 set back or flare screens on the back side of the zone (figure 4).

Points of Emphasis

When facing a zone, the goal is to reverse the ball and take advantage of the zone shifts and gaps. The 4 must read that the defense is in a zone and find the gap in the middle.

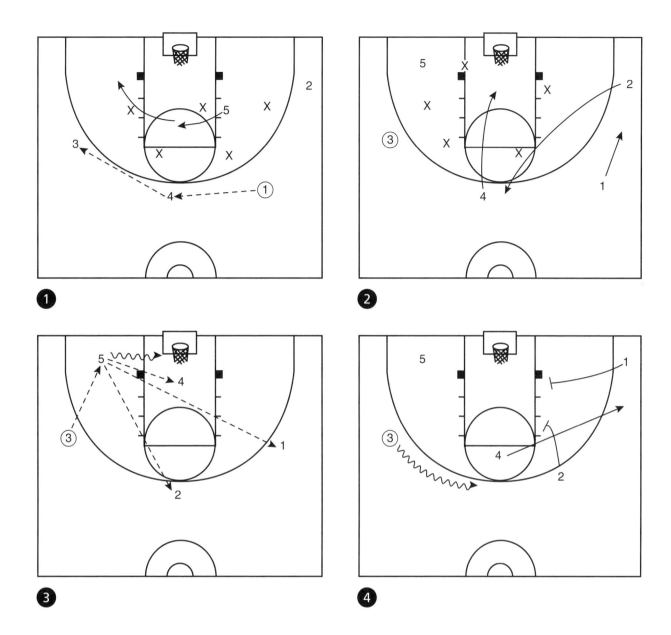

K-FLEX

Tom Collen

Objective

To get 3 an open layup or 5 a post-up opportunity in the lane.

When to Use

- As a secondary offense when a team doesn't have numbers in transition.
- As a called play or an entrance into another offense.
- Against a man-to-man defense.

Key Personnel

Your 3 needs to be a guard who can score inside. Your 5 and 3 must set and use screens well.

Execution

1. In transition, 2 fills the right lane, 3 fills the left lane, and 4 fills the middle. 1 pushes the ball on the dribble and passes it ahead to 2 only if 2 is set and ready to score. 5 trails (see *Kansas*, figure 1, p. 28).

2. 4 sets a high ball screen for 1 driving across the top of the circle. 5 sprints to screen for 3, who cuts across the lane toward the basket (figure 1).

3. After driving off 4's screen, 1 passes the ball back to 4. 2 steps up to the wing, ready for a three-point shot and preventing her defender from helping on 3's flex cut (figure 2).

4. 1 moves down to the free-throw line extended area. 4 looks for 3 on the flex cut (figure 3).

Variations

- If 4 sees 5's defender helping on 3's cut, or if the defenders for 5 and 3 switch, then 4 either passes to 1 or 5, who might be open for a pass (figure 4).
- If 5's defender stays to help with 3, 5 posts up in the lane for the pass from 1.

Points of Emphasis

The 3 can't allow her defender to body over the screen and allow 5's defender to stay close to 5. The wing players must fade low enough on the wings to make a post-entry pass short and quick. If 5 isn't getting the screen set soon enough, 5 might need to start on the weak-side post, thus being closer to 3 and setting the screen on 3's defender sooner.

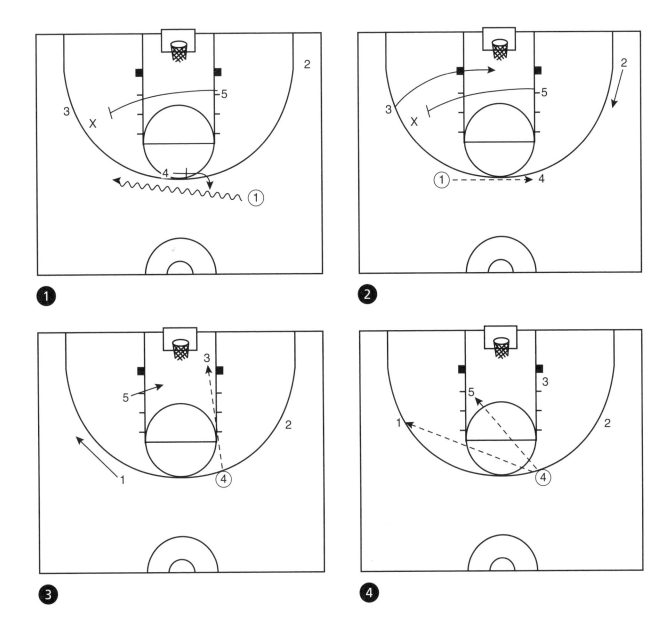

PRIMARY BREAK

Doug Bruno

Objective

To create an easy layup in transition.

When to Use

Following any change in possession—turnover, steal, rebound, or made basket.

Key Personnel

The play will work regardless of personnel on the floor, but all players must be committed to sprinting down the court and taking care of the basketball.

Execution

1. 1 breaks to the free-throw line on the opponent's side of the court to receive the ball from the player who created the break, in this case 5. 2 sprints to the dead right corner, 3 sprints to the dead left corner, 4 sprints to the right block, and 5 trails as 1 pushes the ball upcourt (figure 1).

2. As soon as possible after 1 crosses half-court, 1 passes the ball to 2, who shoots the three-pointer or passes quickly to 4 for the layup (figure 2).

Points of Emphasis

A break can start at any time, with players in any position. Thus it's imperative that each player knows how to fill each position. Players should push the ball up the floor, share the ball, and capitalize on the quick layup.

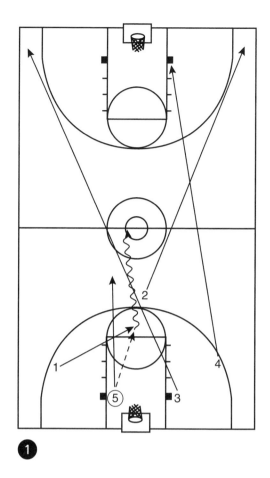

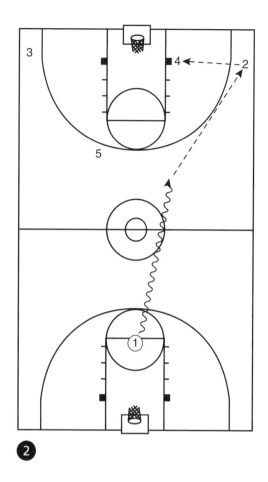

WEAK-SIDE DRIVE

Doug Bruno

Objective

To create an open scoring opportunity when the defense is out of position.

When to Use

Any time the defense is lagging in their transition from fast-break defense to half-court defense.

Key Personnel

The play will work regardless of personnel on the floor, but all players must commit to sprinting down the court and taking care of the basketball.

Execution

1. 1 breaks to the free-throw line on the opponent's side of the court to receive the ball from the player who created the break, in this case 5. 2 sprints to the dead right corner, 3 sprints to the dead left corner, 4 sprints to the right block, and 5 trails as 1 pushes the ball upcourt (see *Primary Break*, figure 1, p. 41).

2. 1 drives from the right side to the left-side top of the key, with 5 cutting behind her to set a screen for 2 on the right wing. 3 pops out to the left wing as 1 continues driving to midway down the lane on the left side. 1 passes to 3 (figure 1).

3. 3 dribbles toward the top of the key and passes as soon as possible to 2 coming off 5's screen. 1 and 5 pop out to their respective wings (figure 2).

4. 2 dribbles to the left. 3 v-cuts to get open for the pass on the high wing, which 1 vacated by sprinting to the elbow and cutting low (figure 3).

5. 3 dribbles toward the top of the key and then passes to 2, who uses another screen by 5 to get open on the wing as 1 pops to the left wing and 4 pops to the left block (figure 4).

Points of Emphasis

If the defense is caught out of position in transitioning from their primary break defense into their half-court defense, a shot can be taken at any time during the secondary break.

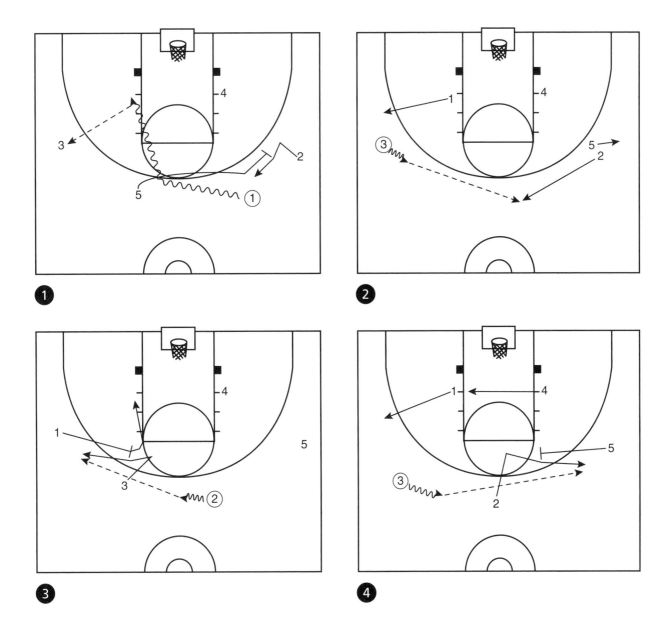

WEAK-SIDE PASS

Doug Bruno

Objective

To create an open scoring opportunity when the defense is out of position.

When to Use

Any time the defense is lagging in their transition from fast-break defense to half-court defense.

Key Personnel

The play will work regardless of personnel on the floor, but all players must commit to sprinting down the court and taking care of the basketball.

Execution

1. 1 breaks to the free-throw line on the opponent's side of the court to receive the ball from the player who created the break, in this case 5. 2 sprints to the dead right corner, 3 sprints to the dead left corner, 4 sprints to the right block, and 5 trails as 1 pushes the ball upcourt (see *Primary Break*, figure 1, p. 41).

2. 1 passes to 2 on the right-side wing and then drops to the right corner as the ball is reversed from 2 to 5 and then 3 on the left wing (figure 1).

3. 1 uses a stagger screen from 2 and 5 to get free at the top of the key and receive the ball from 3 (figure 2).

4. 5 screens for 2, who receives the pass from 1 (figure 3).

5. 2 dribbles toward the top of the key and passes to 1, who v-cuts out to the left wing off a screen by 4. 4 returns to the left block as 3 drops to the corner (figure 4).

6. 1 dribbles toward the left lane line extended and passes to 2, who uses a screen from 5 to get open on the right wing (figure 5).

Points of Emphasis

If the defense is caught out of position in transitioning from their primary break defense into their half-court defense, a shot can be taken at any time during the secondary break.

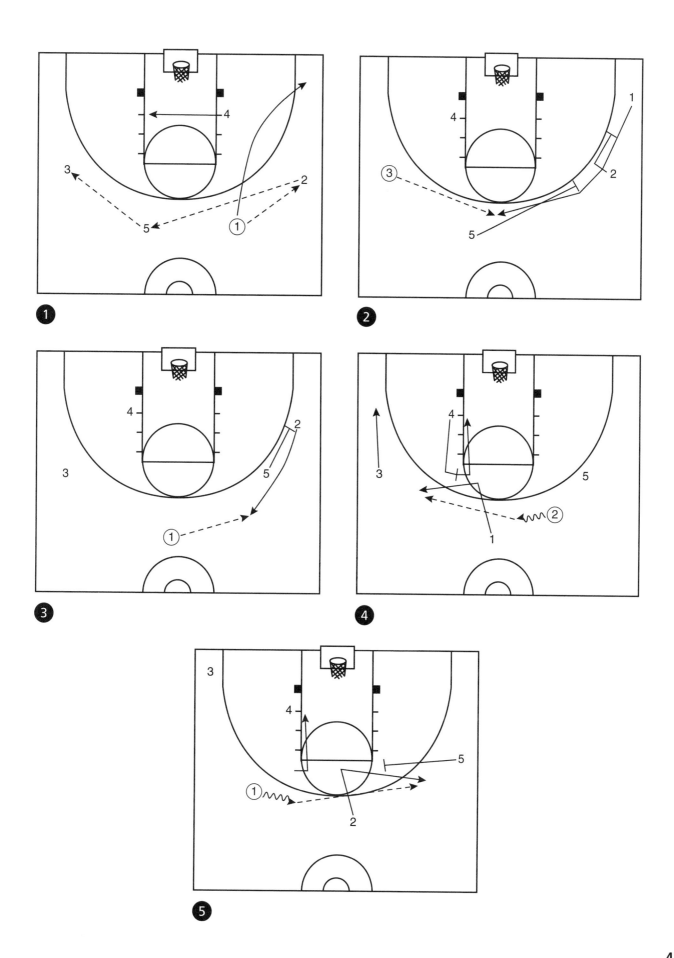

STRONG-SIDE PASS

Doug Bruno

Objective

To create an open scoring opportunity when the defense is out of position.

When to Use

Any time the defense is lagging in their transition from fast-break defense to half-court defense.

Key Personnel

The play will work regardless of personnel on the floor, but all players must commit to sprinting down the court and taking care of the basketball.

Execution

1. 1 breaks to the free-throw line on the opponent's side of the court to receive the ball from the player who created the break, in this case 5. 2 sprints to the dead right corner, 3 sprints to the dead left corner, 4 sprints to the right block, and 5 trails as 1 pushes the ball upcourt (see *Primary Break*, figure 1, p. 41).

2. 1 passes to 2 on the right wing and then sets the beginning of a stagger screen with 5 on the left wing for 3, who cuts to the top of the key (figure 1).

3. 2 passes to 3, who passes to 1 after 1 uses 5's screen to v-cut to above the arc (figure 2).

4. 1 dribbles toward the top of the key and passes to 3, who v-cuts off 4's screen at the right elbow to get open on the wing as 2 drops to the corner. 4 returns to the block (figure 3).

5. 3 dribbles to the top of the key and passes to 1, who v-cuts off 5's screen at the left elbow to get open (figure 4).

Points of Emphasis

If the defense is caught out of position in transitioning from their primary break defense into their half-court defense, a shot can be taken at any time during the secondary break.

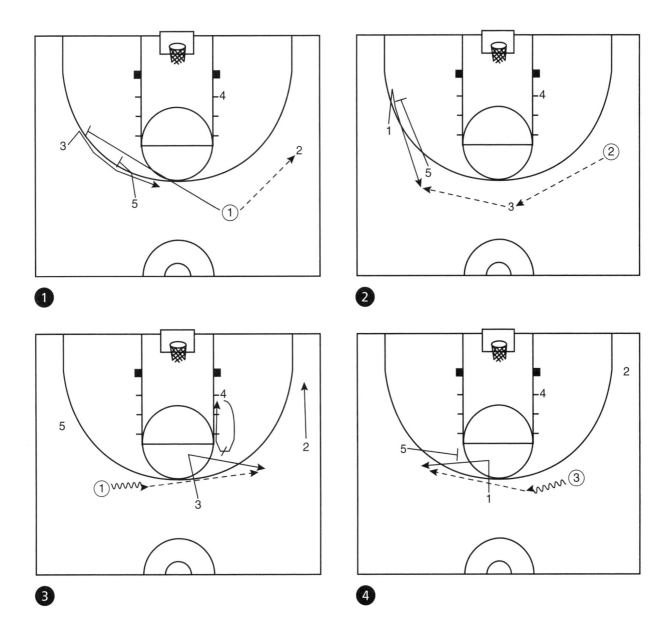

TRAIL POST PASS

Doug Bruno

Objective

To create an open scoring opportunity when the defense is out of position.

When to Use

Any time the defense is lagging in their transition from fast-break defense to half-court defense.

Key Personnel

The play will work regardless of personnel on the floor, but all players must commit to sprinting down the court and taking care of the basketball.

Execution

1. 1 breaks to the free-throw line on the opponent's side of the court to receive the ball from the player who created the break, in this case 5. 2 sprints to the dead right corner, 3 sprints to the dead left corner, 4 sprints to the right block, and 5 trails as 1 pushes the ball upcourt (see *Primary Break*, figure 1, p. 41).

2. 1 passes to 5 at the top of the key as 2 runs off 4's screen and along the baseline to the left side (figure 1).

3. 5 dribbles back right and passes to 1, who v-cuts off 4's screen to get open on the right wing. 4 drops to the block (figure 2).

4. 2 uses a stagger screen set by 3 and 5 to receive the pass from 1 at the top of the key (figure 3).

5. 5 then screens for 3, who pops up to receive the pass from 2 (figure 4).

6. 3 dribbles toward the top of the key and passes to 2, who v-cuts off 4's screen to get open on the right wing as 1 drops to the corner. 4 returns to the block (figure 5).

7. 2 dribbles toward the top of the key and passes to 3, who v-cuts off 5's screen to get open on the wing (figure 6).

Points of Emphasis

If the defense is caught out of position in transitioning from their primary break defense into their half-court defense, a shot can be taken at any time during the secondary break.

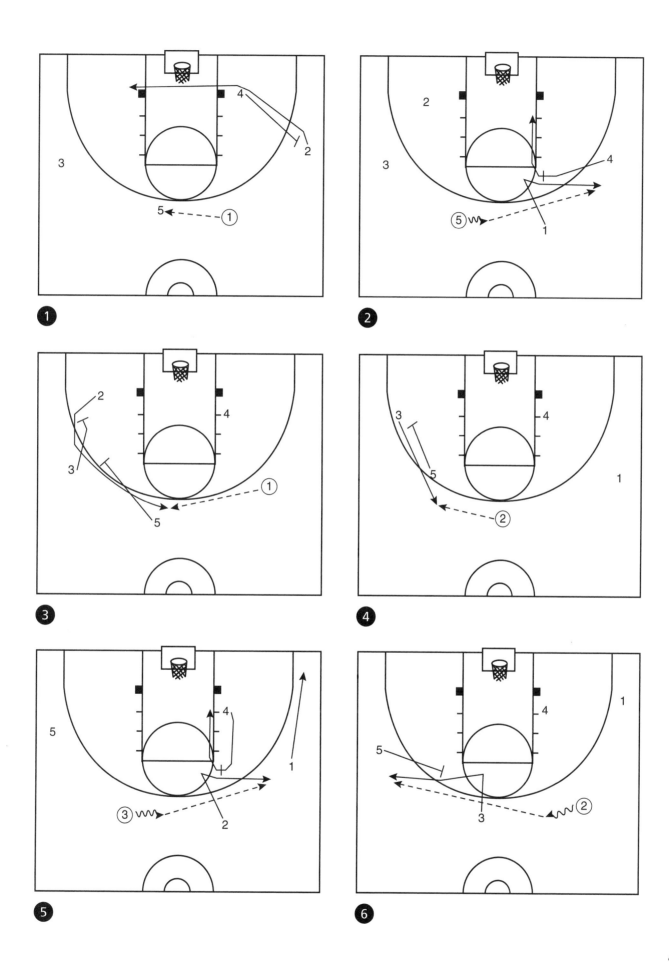

CLEAR 1

Quentin Hillsman

Objective

To create an open-floor situation for a player to drive to the basket for a high-percentage shot.

When to Use

Against an opponent with matchup problems in man-to-man defense.

Key Personnel

This set is very effective for a team that plays well off the bounce, has great movement, and can play drive-and-kick basketball.

Execution

1. 5 back-screens for 2, who clears to the weak side (figure 1).
2. 5 slip-screens for 1 and then breaks to the ball-side elbow. 3 and 4 set a stagger screen for 2 on the weak side for movement and then pop back out to the perimeter to clear the lane. 1 attacks the rim (figure 2).

Points of Emphasis

Each player must move simultaneously as 1 starts her dribble entry. The four players without the ball create movement and space away from the ball with screens and hard cuts. If players are stationary on the weak side, defenders might drop down and clog the path to the rim. At the same time, players should make themselves available and visible for catch-and-shoot and drive-and-kick opportunities as 1 attacks the rim.

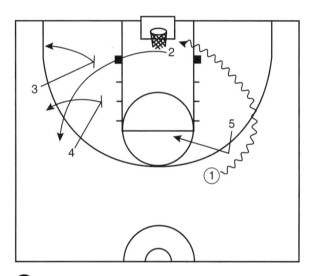

CLEAR 2

Quentin Hillsman

Objective

To create an open-floor situation for a player to drive to the basket for a high-percentage shot.

When to Use

Against an opponent with matchup problems in man-to-man defense.

Key Personnel

This set is very effective for a team that plays well off the bounce, has great movement, and can play drive-and-kick basketball.

Execution

1. 1 dribbles to the left side of the key extended. 2 uses a stagger screen from 4 (in the middle of the key) and 5 (on the right-side wing) to get clear to receive the ball on the right wing (figure 1).

2. 3 drops to the left corner, 4 pops out to left wing, and 5 steps to the left elbow or midpost (depending on her shooting range) as 1 passes the ball to 2, who attacks the rim (figure 2).

Variation

If 1 can't pass to 2, 1 can dribble to 2 and hand the ball off before continuing to the right corner.

Points of Emphasis

Each player must move simultaneously as 1 starts her dribble entry. The four players without the ball create movement and space away from the ball with screens and hard cuts. If players are stationary on the weak side, defenders might drop down and clog the path to the rim. At the same time, players should make themselves available and visible for catch-and-shoot and drive-and-kick opportunities as 1 attacks the rim.

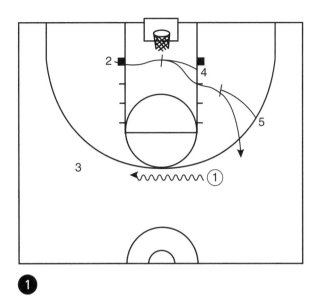

1

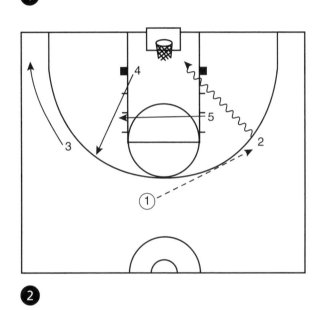

2

CLEAR 3

Quentin Hillsman

Objective

To create an open-floor situation for a player to drive to the basket for a high-percentage shot.

When to Use

Against an opponent with matchup problems in man-to-man defense.

Key Personnel

This set is very effective for a team that plays well off the bounce, has great movement, and can play drive-and-kick basketball.

Execution

1. 1 dribbles to the left side of the key extended. 2 runs the baseline to the left corner. 3 shallow-cuts to the right wing. 4 floats to the left wing. 5 pops to the left midpost or elbow, depending on her shooting range (figure 1).

2. 1 passes to 3, who attacks the rim (figure 2).

Variation

If 1 can't pass to 3, she can dribble to 3 and hand the ball off before continuing to the right corner.

Points of Emphasis

Each player must move simultaneously as 1 starts her dribble entry. The four players without the ball create movement and space away from the ball with screens and hard cuts. If players are stationary on the weak side, defenders might drop down and clog the path to the rim. At the same time, players should make themselves available and visible for catch-and-shoot and drive-and-kick opportunities as 1 attacks the rim.

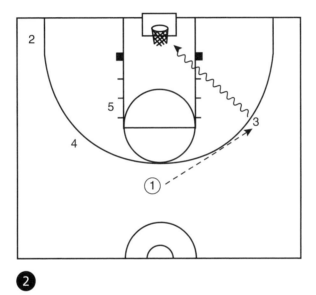

CLEAR 4

Quentin Hillsman

Objective

To create an open-floor situation for a player to drive to the basket for a high-percentage shot.

When to Use

Against an opponent with matchup problems in man-to-man defense.

Key Personnel

This set is very effective for a team that plays well off the bounce, has great movement, and can play drive-and-kick basketball.

Execution

1. 1 dribbles to the left side of the key extended as 3 drops to left dead corner. 4 shallow-cuts to the right wing, 2 shallow-cuts to left wing, and 5 pops to the left midpost or elbow, depending on her shooting range (figure 1).
2. 1 passes to 4, who attacks the rim (figure 2).

Variation

If 1 can't pass to 4, she can dribble to 4 and hand the ball off before continuing to the right corner.

Points of Emphasis

Each player must move simultaneously as 1 starts her dribble entry. The four players without the ball create movement and space away from the ball with screens and hard cuts. If players are stationary on the weak side, defenders might drop down and clog the path to the rim. At the same time, players should make themselves available and visible for catch-and-shoot and drive-and-kick opportunities as 1 attacks the rim.

1

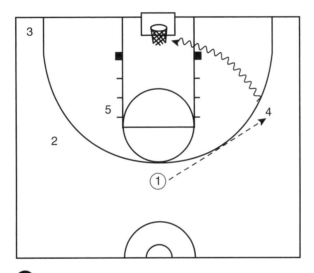

2

CLEAR 5

Quentin Hillsman

Objective

To create an open-floor situation for a player to drive to the basket for a high-percentage shot.

When to Use

Against an opponent with matchup problems in man-to-man defense.

Key Personnel

This set is very effective for a team that plays well off the bounce, has great movement, and can play drive-and-kick basketball.

Execution

1. 1 dribbles to the left side of the key extended. 2 heads to the basket and then cuts to the left elbow. 3 drops to the dead left corner, and 4 takes her place on the left wing. 5 pops out to the right wing (figure 1).
2. 1 passes the ball to 5, who attacks the rim (figure 2).

Variation

If 1 can't pass the ball to 5, she can dribble to 5 and hand the ball off before continuing to the right corner.

Points of Emphasis

Each player must move simultaneously as 1 starts her dribble entry. The four players without the ball create movement and space away from the ball with screens and hard cuts. If players are stationary on the weak side, defenders might drop down and clog the path to the rim. At the same time, players should make themselves available and visible for catch-and-shoot and drive-and-kick opportunities as 1 attacks the rim.

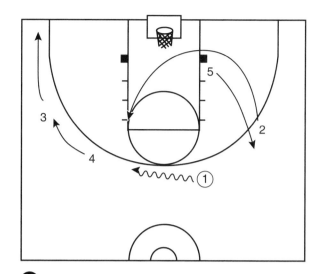

1

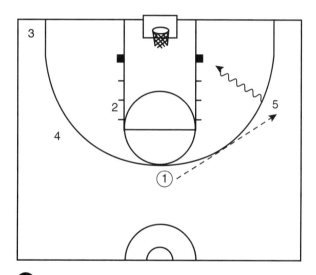

2

CHAPTER

3

Post Plays vs. Man-to-Man Defense

A must for any team's offense is an arsenal of plays to get the ball into the hands of your post players. In getting the ball to your inside players you can create high-percentage shot opportunities, feed a hot hand, take advantage of a size or ability mismatch inside, isolate a player for a one-on-one matchup, attack a defender in foul trouble, hide a weak perimeter game (or player), and free up guards being smothered defensively.

When an inside game is working, your offense is easy and effective, predictable yet unstoppable. After a few successful post plays, a team feeds on the momentum on both ends of the court, and the opponent must make adjustments to keep the game from getting out of control.

But playing against a man-to-man defense is not easy. Doing so requires players to set, read, and use screens properly and with good timing and to make a variety of purposeful, believable cuts to shake defenders. At least one post player must be strong inside, and if you have two such players, they can work together to create additional options with the high-low game.

Patience in a post game is a must. Defenses rarely break down on the first, second, or even the third pass. Offenses that pass the ball crisply, read the movement and options quickly and accurately, and wait for the moment the defense is out of position to pounce will thrive because eventually a defender will become lazy or distracted, get caught in a screen, or find herself sealed away from the ball.

Just because an offense is post oriented doesn't mean the guards aren't important to its execution. Perimeter players must be proficient at reading the defense, setting screens, and passing the ball. Beyond that, in order to truly open up the middle, at least one perimeter player must be a threat from the outside. Otherwise, defenders can pack the lane, double- or triple-teaming a dominant post player to no ill effect.

61

Keep in mind that any of the plays in this book can be modified to fit your team's personnel and abilities. It's important for coaches to design and then call plays that bring out the strengths of their players. Similarly, players on the court must recognize the strengths of the post players and focus on the options within the play that cater to those strengths. For example, running a lob-pass play inside to a post player who's more brawn than finesse will rarely produce points.

STAGGER SCREEN AWAY

Lisa Bluder

Objective

To clear out the weak-side defense and get a post player a good lob pass or a one-on-one opportunity.

When to Use

- When a post player needs to be more involved in a game or needs a confidence boost.
- In transition.

Key Personnel

This play requires a guard with good passing skills and a post who can score.

Execution

1 passes ahead to 2 as she v-cuts to get open. 2 looks inside at 5 posting hard. If the defense is fronting, 2 lobs a pass. If the defense is on 5's back, 2 makes a direct pass. In the meantime, 1 and 4 set stagger screens away for 3, who looks to shoot off the pass if 2 can't get the ball inside (see the figure).

Point of Emphasis

The 3 sets her defense up as high as possible, making it tough for defenders to help.

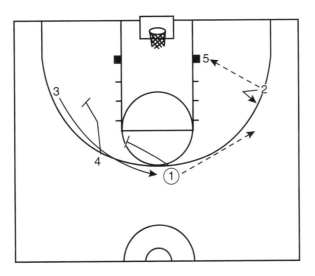

PIN-LOB

Cristy McKinney

Objective

To get a quick-hit lob to the post player.

When to Use

When a quick basket is needed.

Key Personnel

The post player needs good hands and the ability to receive a lob pass. The 1 must be able to execute the lob pass.

Execution

1. 1 goes off a screen from 5. 4 ducks in hard to the basket, and 2 looks for a pass in the corner for a shot (figure 1).
2. 3 cuts in and back-screens for 5, who goes to the basket. 1 lobs to 5 for a score (figure 2).

Points of Emphasis

The lob is the primary play, but if 4 ducks in hard and is open, she should take advantage of her great position. The back screen from 3 must be solid, and 1 must be ready to deliver the pass to 5.

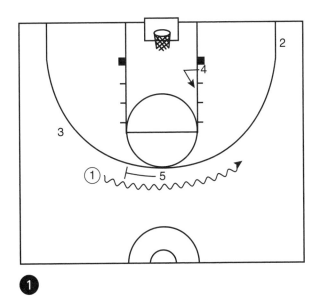

1

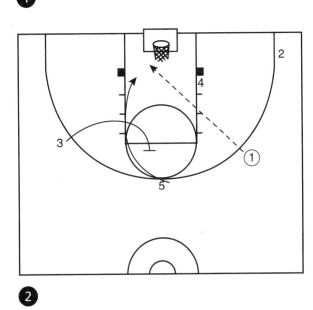

2

2

Cristy McKinney

Objective

To get a jumper from the wing or a quick hit inside to a post player.

When to Use

When you need a good look for a two-point basket, getting a wing a touch while also setting up a post player to work hard for a good look at the basket.

Key Personnel

Your 3 player must shoot well from the corner. Your 2 player should be able to read defenses. Your 4 player must be able to set a good screen and roll back to the ball.

Execution

1. 1 dribbles to the left wing, using 4's screen, if desired—unless the defense traps, in which case she shouldn't use the screen. 3 pops hard to the corner, looking for a shot, and 5 steps toward the basket and then pops back out to receive a pass from 1 (figure 1).

2. On the pass from 1 to 5, 2 heads to the bucket and then breaks off a screen from 4, who opens to the ball. 2 reads the defense, looking for a jumper, curl, or fade. 5 looks for 2 coming off the screen or 4 rolling back to the ball (figure 2).

3. If 2 receives the pass with no scoring opportunity, she dribbles to the wing while looking for 4. At the same time, 1 and 5 set stagger screens for 3, who comes hard to the top of the key looking for a pass from 2 (figure 3).

Variations

- If defenders cheat over the top on the screen for 2, a quick pass to 2 under the basket can result in a layup.
- Also, 2 can look for a pass over the top if 5 slips or rolls after screening for 3.

Points of Emphasis

Decision making and good timing are critical when running this play, and all players must work to set, read, and use screens correctly. If executed properly, it's difficult for a defense to take away every option, providing post players good looks if they roll back hard to the ball and work to seal in the paint. The 2 player must put her head under the basket to set up the screen and be committed to coming off the screen first. Only on an overplay does she look to get the quick pass under the basket. Weak-side action helps keep the defense occupied as scoring chances occur on the strong side. But players should be patient and not force things on the strong side because 3 coming off the stagger screens might have a good look as well.

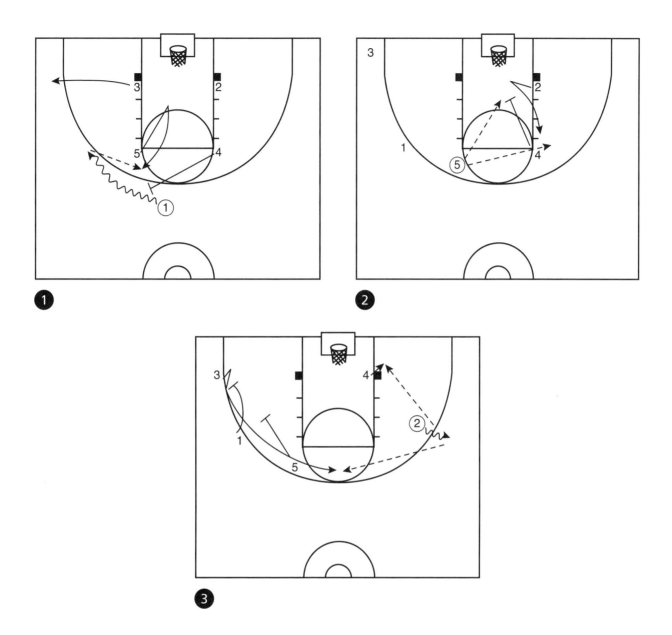

LOW

Cristy McKinney

Objective

To enable two post players to work together to capitalize on post-ups or high-low action.

When to Use

When a team has an inside advantage over its opponents, especially when 4 isn't a strong perimeter player.

Key Personnel

The two post players work together to create scoring opportunities using screens. The guards space the floor, read the defense, make good passes, and stay ready for kick-outs.

Execution

1. 1 passes to 2 on the right wing and cuts to the ball-side corner. On the pass, 4 screens across for 5, who pops to the ball-side elbow (figure 1).
2. 4 rolls back hard to the ball, looking for the pass. If it's not there, 2 passes to 5 (figure 2).
3. 4 pins her defender and looks for a lob from 5, who's also looking to shoot or attack the basket (figure 3).
4. If nothing is available, 5 passes to 3. On the pass, 4 sets a flex screen for 1, who cuts across to the opposite corner. 5 then steps toward 3, gets a good angle, and down-screens for 4. The continuity continues, with 3 now looking for 4 at the elbow or 5 on the low block (figure 4).

Variations

- If defenders cheat on the post screen, the post being screened can go to the block rather than the elbow.
- Also, the pass to the wing is an opportunity for a drive-and-kick to the corner.

Points of Emphasis

A flex screen is a screen set on the baseline, bringing an offensive player from one corner to the other. The screener faces the sideline, and the cutter uses the screen to get open. This continuity offense allows for post players who work together to get looks inside. Posts need to be aware that if the defense switches, they should roll back to the ball and be open.

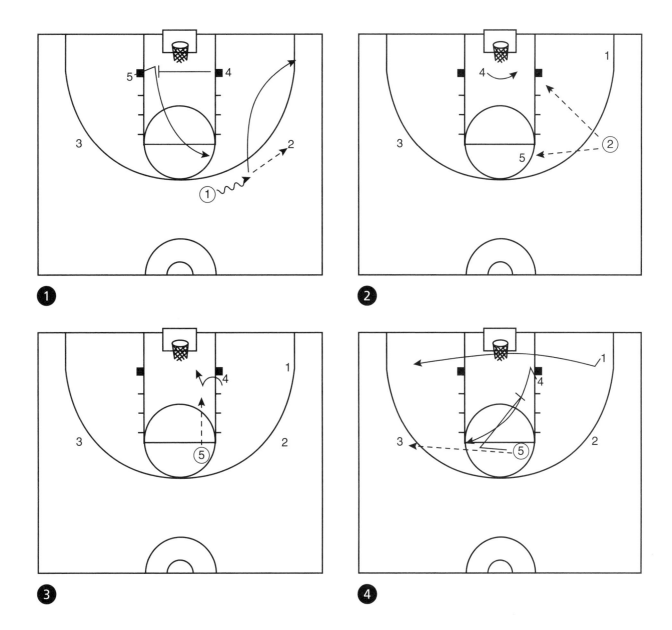

SWING

Cristy McKinney

Objective

To get an isolation in the post.

When to Use

- When an opponent is mismatched inside.
- When a post player has a hot hand.
- When a quick score is needed.

Key Personnel

Your 5 player should be able to score with her back to the basket. Perimeter players should be able to shoot in case of a double team inside.

Execution

1. 1 dribbles to the right side. 4 pops up the lane to above the elbow. 1 passes to 4 (figure 1).
2. 2 cuts hard through the lane to the opposite corner, looking to distract 5's defender. 5 ducks in hard, looking for a pass from 4 (figure 2).
3. If the pass is unavailable, 4 passes back to 1, who looks for 5 sealing her defender in the paint. 1 passes to 5, who has a one-on-one opportunity at the basket (figure 3).
4. If 5 is double-teamed from the weak side, she kicks the ball out to 2 or 3. If the double comes from the strong side, 1 relocates, looking for the pass (figure 4).

Variation

If opponents deny the entry pass into the post, 4 must be able to shoot or drive from the elbow after allowing 2 to clear to the corner. If either defender sags to help on 4, 2 and 5 should be ready for the pass. The play can be run to either side.

Points of Emphasis

The 2 must be sure to get a piece of 5's defender so 5 can get a step into the middle. Many times the pass won't come from 4 but from 1. Timing is key. The 2 shouldn't cut through until the pass is made from 1 to 4.

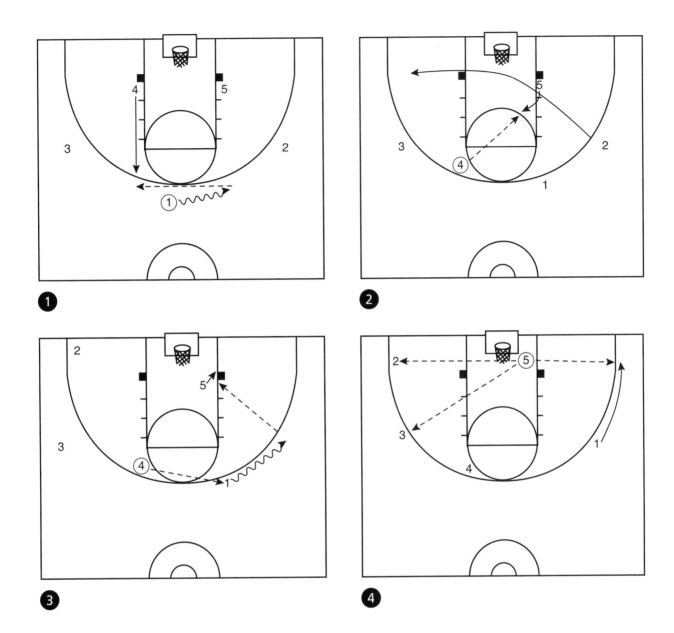

TIGER

Cristy McKinney

Objective

To get a quick hit inside or weave action for a score.

When to Use

When a team has an advantage on the block, superior athleticism, and an ability to read the defense.

Key Personnel

A strong post presence is important, but quickness and good passing on the perimeter are also necessary for this play to succeed.

Execution

1. 1 dribbles to the left wing, pushing 3 to the corner. 5 posts hard, and 4 flashes up the lane to the elbow. 2 pops to the top of the key (figure 1).

2. 1 looks for a quick entry to 5 but otherwise hits either 2 or 4. If 2 gets the ball, she can either use a ball screen from 4 and attack the basket or pass to 4 and rub by 4 for a handoff on the basket side. As 2 rubs off 4, 1 screens to get 3 back to the wing (figure 2).

3. If 2 does not receive the handoff, she goes to the block as 4 dribbles toward 3 to hand off the ball. On the handoff, 2 screens across for 5 and then 4 down-screens for 2, who pops to the top. 3 drives to the wing and looks to pass to 5 or 2 for the shot (figure 3).

Variation

To isolate for a quick drive, 4 can flash to the elbow where she might have a side cleared for a drive or shot.

Points of Emphasis

For optimal spacing, 4 stays on the elbow opposite the ball. The timing of the handoffs and the cuts is very important.

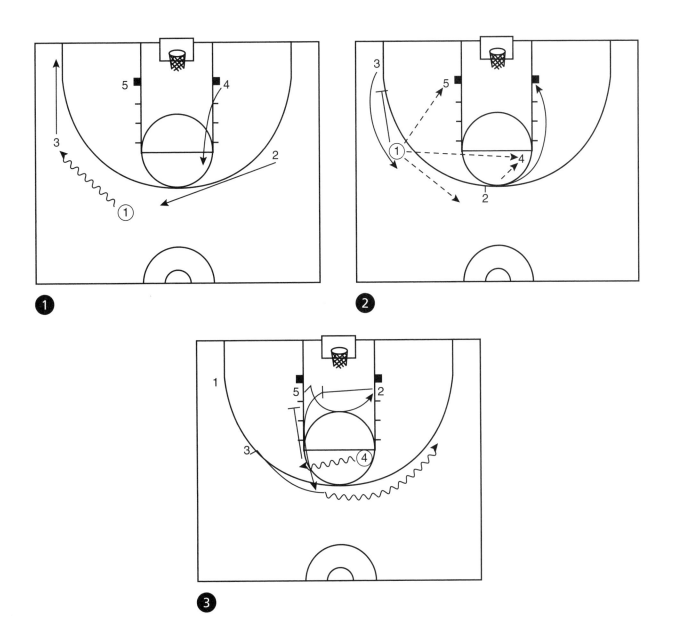

DOUBLE CROSS

Kathy Miller

Objectives

- To isolate your best low-post player one on one on the block.
- To force your best shooter's defender to help on a back screen, freeing up your best shooter to knock down an elbow jumper.

When to Use

- When a low-post defender is ineffective.
- When a low-post defender is in foul trouble.

Key Personnel

Your 4 needs to shoot well from the perimeter so her defender can't sag and help with the low post. The 4 must also make good passes and decisions with the basketball. Your 2 must shoot well from the outside and make quick reads and decisions. Most important, your 5 must be able to score or draw a foul and, preferably, be a player opponents feel they must double-team.

Execution

1. 5 cross-screens 4 at the right elbow so 4 can cut to the left wing. At the same time, 2 takes a step inside the key and screens for 3, who moves to the left corner. 1 passes to 4 on the left wing (figure 1).

2. After the pass, 2 sets an angled back screen for 5 to the left block and then reverse pivots on her outside foot and opens up to the basketball as she pops to the elbow. If 5's defender is playing behind, 4 passes immediately to 5. If 5's defender is playing in front, 4 skips to 2. 1 holds. 2 can shoot the open jumper from the elbow or hit 5 in the low post (figure 2).

Points of Emphasis

The 4 should wait to be screened—better to be late to a screen than early—and then cut over the top of it. The 5 then cuts underneath the screen, trying to get a layup and forcing 2's defender to help. On the skip pass, 5 aggressively seals her defender and lets the ball find her instead of following its flight. The pass from 2 to 5 needs to be crisp.

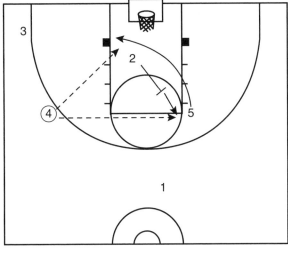

1

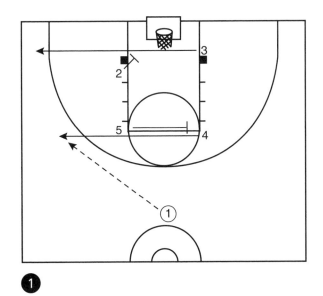

2

5 BACK

Lisa Bluder

Objective

To take advantage of a defender who really shows high or hedges on on-ball screens, forcing the ball handler to dribble back instead of going shoulder to shoulder with the screener.

When to Use

When teams show high when defending on-ball screens.

Key Personnel

The point guard should be able to use an on-ball screen and make a lob pass. The off-guard needs to set good screens. The post will need to screen, catch, and convert.

Execution

1. 1 dribbles off 5's on-ball screen to the left wing while 4 cuts off 2's screen on the baseline (figure 1).
2. 3 circles around and creates a good angle to set a back screen for 5, who cuts for a lob pass from 1 (figure 2).

Points of Emphasis

The 3 needs to make sure she cuts low enough to get a good angle on the back screen so that 5 is open for a lob pass.

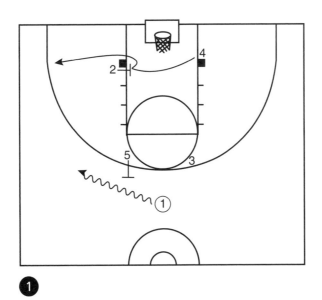

1

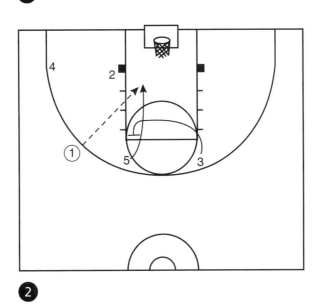

2

BACK DOWN

Lisa Bluder

Objective

To get a shot for the post diving to the basket or for a shooter at the top of the key.

When to Use

- When the post defender is struggling or in foul trouble.
- When a three-point shot is needed.

Key Personnel

Your 5 must be a solid post player. Your 2 should be accurate from behind the arc. Your 1 must be an accurate passer.

Execution

1. 1 dribbles to the left side, using an on-ball screen by 4 if desired or necessary. 2 sets a diagonal back screen for 5, who cuts hard to the block for the pass (figure 1).
2. 4 screens down for 2, who looks for a pass from 1 for the three-point shot (figure 2).

Variation

This play can be run to either side with equal effectiveness.

Points of Emphasis

The 4 needs to wait and have good timing when setting the screen for 2. If not, she walks her defender down and clogs up the paint as 2 is setting the screen on 5.

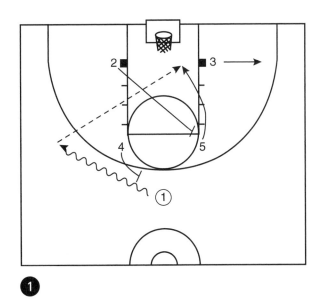

1

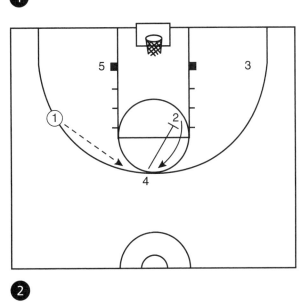

2

HIGH-LOW

Lisa Bluder

Objective

To clear out the weak-side defense and isolate the post for a one-on-one move.

When to Use

- When the post is scoring at will or has a height advantage.
- When the defending post is struggling or in foul trouble.

Key Personnel

Your 5 should have a reliable shot. Your 4 needs good passing ability and must also be a threat from the outside so the defense can't sag off her.

Execution

1. 1 passes to 2 and cuts to the corner. 4 flashes to the area between the free-throw line and three-point line (figure 1).
2. 4 receives the pass from 2 and passes to 5, who's flashing into the paint (figure 2).

Points of Emphasis

The 4 should time her flash so that she's catching on the move. The 5 needs to get a good seal on her defender when 2 has the ball, so she can then pin her when the ball is passed to 4.

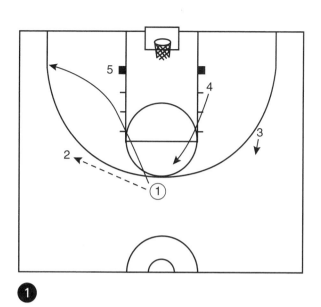

1

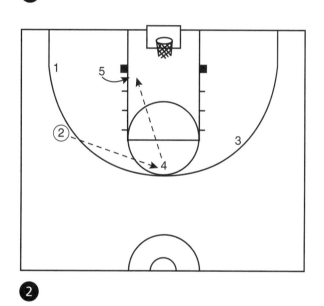

2

ON-BALL CROSS

Lisa Bluder

Objective

To create a shot for the post or for a three-point shooter.

When to Use

- When a three-point shot is needed.
- When the post needs a good touch to take a high-percentage shot from good position.

Key Personnel

Your 5 must be a scorer, and your 2 requires good range.

Execution

1. 1 dribbles to the left wing, using an on-ball screen at the top of the key by 4. 2 cross-screens for 5, who flashes across (figure 1).
2. 5 looks for the pass and shot. 4 sets a down screen for 2 as she comes up for the three-point shot (figure 2).

Points of Emphasis

The timing on the 2-to-5 screen is important. The 2 should go screen as 1 is coming off 4's on-ball screen. It's also important for 2 to set a good screen on 5. The more 5's defender must help on the post, the better look 5 will get at the basket.

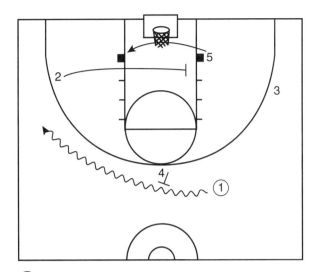

1

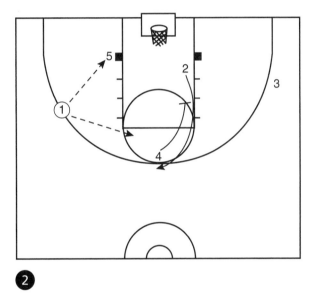

2

14

Agnus Berenato

Objective

To create motion high-low for the inside game.

When to Use

Against a man-to-man defense.

Key Personnel

Your 5 must be a scorer on the low block. Your 4 can shoot the 15-footer or put the ball on the floor. Both should be strong with the ball and able to make the high-low pass into the post. Guards must be strong on the wings.

Execution

1. 2 and 3 use screens from 4 and 5 to pop out to the wings. 4 flashes high, and 1 passes to 2 (figure 1).

2. 1 screens away for 3, and 2 has three options. The first is hitting 5, who's posting up inside. The second is passing to 4, who looks high-low (figure 2).

3. The third is passing to 3, in which case 4 screens down for 5 and then flashes high, 3 reverses the ball to 1 and then screens for 2, and 5 continues across the lane, following the ball (figure 3).

4. The motion continues as described except with 3 screening for 2 on the opposite side until a seam is found.

Points of Emphasis

The 1 must know which post players are in the game and go to their strengths. For instance, if 4 can shoot the jumper, then 1 runs the play opposite 4 to bring her to the high post. If 5 is excellent on the block, 1 passes through the options so 4 can down-screen to get 5 open low. Either way, 4 and 5 must wait for the screen and stay low. The post who sets the down screen should open up for a quick pass from the guard for a quick score or foul. Once the guard passes into the post on the low block, she looks to relocate for the kick-out.

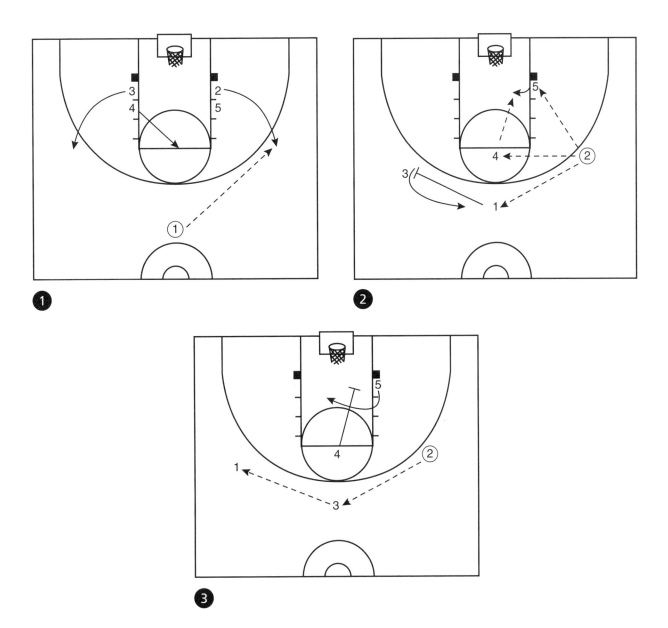

HORNS

Agnus Berenato

Objective

To isolate a great post player on the low block for a score or to free up a guard.

When to Use

Against a man-to-man defense.

Key Personnel

Ideally, 4 and 5 are interchangeable and are effective scorers on the low block and the elbow. The guards should be strong on the wing, able to make a pass into the post and to score off a screen.

Execution

1. 1 dribbles to the right wing, using a ball screen from 4 if necessary or desired. 3 pops out to the left wing, and 2 sets a diagonal back screen for 5 cutting to the ball. 1 looks to hit 5 posting up (figure 1).

2. If that option is not available, 4 down-screens for 2, who comes off the screen at the top of the key looking for a pass from 1 and the shot (figure 2).

3. If the shot isn't there, 5 steps off the block to occupy the defense as 4 sets a ball screen for 2. 2 looks to create an opportunity while 3 spaces to find an opening (figure 3).

4. 4 can open and look for a high-post jump shot or roll to the basket. If 4 rolls, 5 pops high (figure 4).

Points of Emphasis

If she's effective off the dribble, your 1 can look to score off 4's ball-screen. The 2's diagonal back screen must be a good one so 5 can get to the low block and seal off her defender. The 4 must be aware of her defender. If her defender doubles the low-block, 4 makes herself available for the 15-foot jumper.

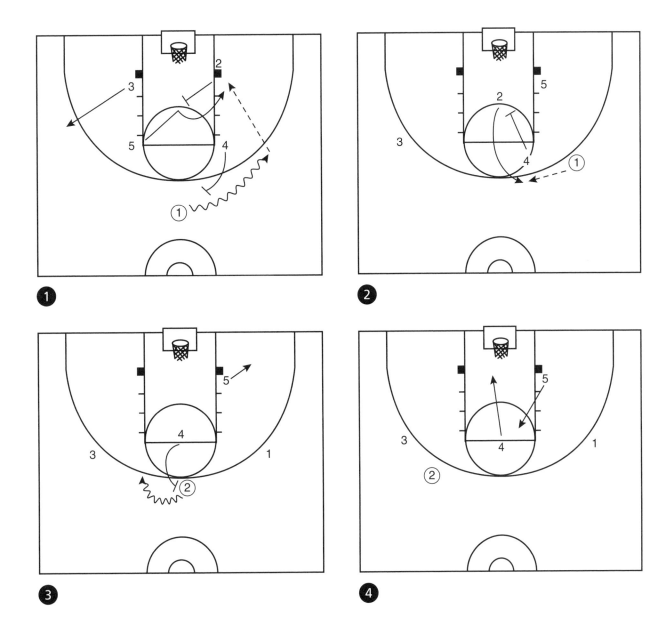

LINDSAY

Agnus Berenato

Objective

To get a post on the low block for an easy bucket.

When to Use

Against a man-to-man defense.

Key Personnel

Your 5 should be an effective scorer on the low block. Your 1 must be able to score off a ball screen in a clear-out situation.

Execution

1. 2 rubs off 3 and pops to the wing as 3 pops to the corner. 1 passes the ball to 2. 4 posts for a 1 count, looking for the ball from 2 (figure 1).

2. If there's no opening, 4 screens for 1, who UCLA cuts to the basket. If 1 is wide open, 2 feeds her the ball for a layup or short jumper. 4 fills the top of the key (figure 2).

3. 2 swings the ball to 3, who looks to score as 1 sets a cross-screen for 5. If nothing's there, 3 reverses back to 2, and 4 down-screens for 1 (figure 3).

4. 2 passes to 1, and 4 sets a ball screen for 1, who looks to take advantage of the clear-out and drives to the basket. 5 reads the defense and looks for pass or "I" cuts (figure 4).

Points of Emphasis

The 5 must wait for the cross-screen from 1 and stay low; the 2 should remember to look for 1 on the UCLA cut. A UCLA cut is when a player cuts to the basket from the top of the key, typically coming off of a screen from the post on the elbow.

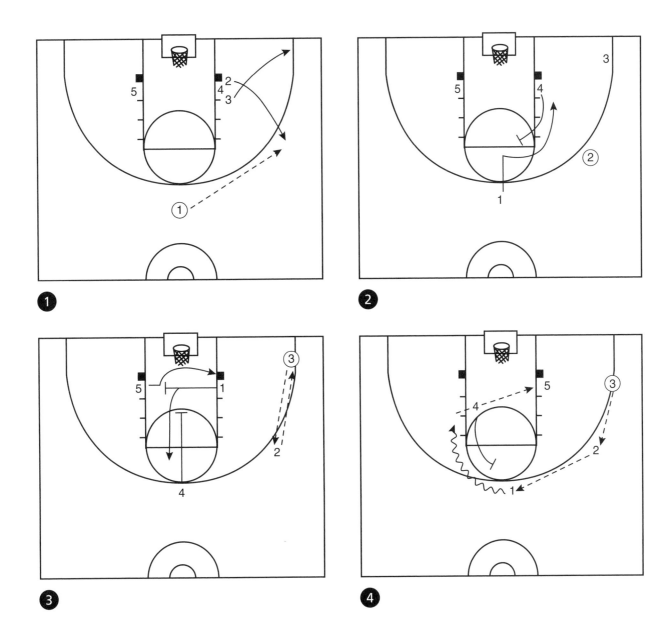

RIDER

Agnus Berenato

Objective

To isolate 4 in the paint.

When to Use

When 4 has a size advantage over her defender.

Key Personnel

Your 4 should be an effective scorer in the paint. Your 2 should be strong enough to post up a smaller guard one on one. Your 5 should be strong on the wing.

Execution

1. 1 dribbles to take 2's place on the right wing as 2 drops to post up her defender (figure 1).
2. 4 steps out above the key to receive a pass from 1. 5 steps out above the key to receive the ball from 4 (figure 2).
3. 4 down-screens for 2. 5 reverses the ball to 2, who feeds 4 low (figure 3).

Points of Emphasis

The 2 looks to score early in the play if she's open on the low block, either inverting and going to the hoop or drop-stepping to score. If not, she waits for the screen from 4, looking to score from the top of the key. Otherwise, 2 must recognize how 4's defender is playing and make the best pass to the post.

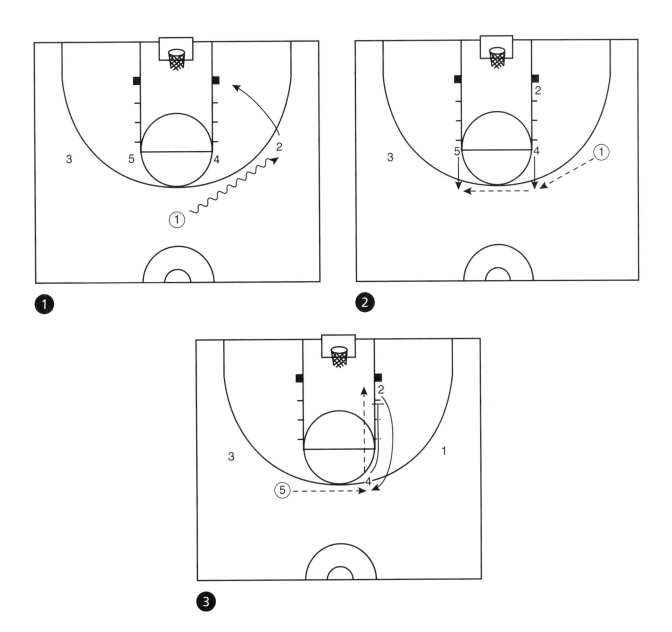

MOTION

Lisa Stone

Objectives

- To free a dominant post.
- To create a mismatch if the defense switches on screens.

When to Use

Against a man-to-man defense.

Key Personnel

You need a dominant post player. Guards should screen well and also be adept at reading and cutting off screens.

Execution

1. 4 sets a ball screen for 1, who dribbles off the screen, looking to attack should opponents defend the screen poorly, or else continues to the right wing. If she continues to the wing, 2 cross-screens for 5, who moves to the strong-side block (figure 1).

2. 4 then down-screens for 2, who cuts up the middle of the lane to above the free-throw line, looking to pass, shoot, or dribble penetrate. 4 rolls back high, looking to receive the ball and feed 5 low (figure 2).

3. If 2 has nothing, 4 ball-screens for 2, who dribbles to the left wing. 3 cross-screens again for 5, then 4 down-screens for 3, and the play continues (figure 3).

Variation

Instead of 3 cross-screening for 5 after the reversal, 4 can ball-screen for 1 at the top and then stay high and receive the pass from 2, allowing 5 to duck in for a pass from 4 (figure 4).

Points of Emphasis

Setting good screens and threatening with the basketball at all times makes this motion offense work. It provides constant small-to-big screens, which discourages a team from switching and thus increases the opportunity for an open look at the basket. But spacing is key. The wider the guards are on the wing, the more room a dominant post player has to work with. Also, it's important for 5 to time her screen and 2 to properly read the screen to dictate whether she shoots, penetrates, or passes.

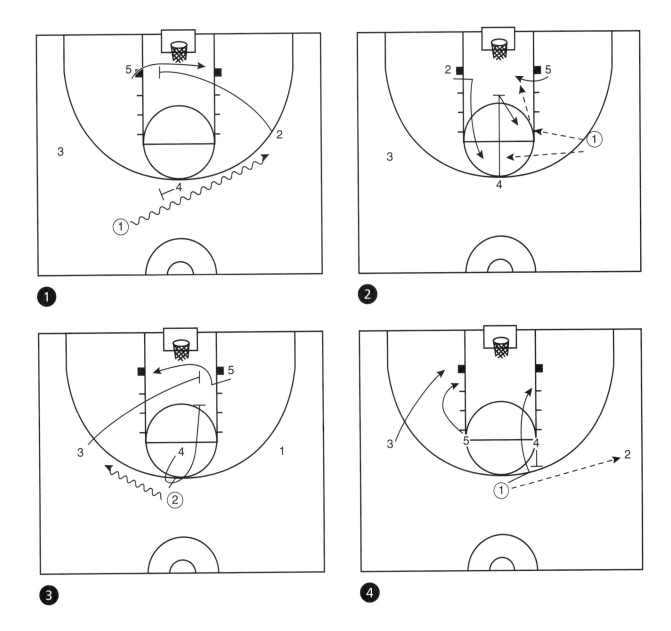

4

Perimeter Plays vs. Man-to-Man Defense

In many respects, it's easier and more productive to defend the inside game with a man-to-man defense than to do so for the outside game. Some offenses tend to force the ball inside, thinking it's their best option, it makes sense for a defense to focus on stopping the higher-percentage shots, and the coverage area is smaller.

When man-to-man defenses are focused on the post play, it should increase the motivation offenses have to perfect perimeter plays against man-to-man coverage. Such plays can create good looks for a star player or a player with a hot hand and open up the inside game by spreading the defense. These plays can put defensive players in positions they aren't used to, confusing them and possibly delaying their reads, leaving an offensive player open.

Plays in this chapter can also counter a variety of tight defenses. Some are designed to slow down defenders who fight through screens with multiple layers and types of screens. Others thwart opponents who instead switch on screens, setting up a speed mismatch that allows a guard to drive past a post player into a relatively empty lane. When teams shift to help on drives, some plays call to kick the ball out to an open perimeter player. All have the potential to punish a team that focuses too much on defending the inside game.

As you would expect, guards must possess a wide range of skills to execute these plays. Depending on the set, they must be able to shoot the jumper and the three-pointer, drive to the basket, post up another player, read the defense and react accordingly, and pass the ball crisply and accurately. Windows of opportunity won't be open long.

But for all players, setting good screens and coming off screens with hard cuts are essential to running these plays effectively. Defenders won't believe that a player jogging through her movements is really going to get the ball. Each offensive player must make her defender believe the play is designed specifically for her. Timeliness is also crucial in using screens well. Unlike arriving at the team bus, it is better to be late to a screen than early. Setting or attempting to use a screen early usually makes the screen ineffective because the play hasn't developed yet.

Also important for running the plays in this chapter are ball movement and player movement. The more quickly and often the ball is passed from one player to another, especially around the perimeter, and the more intensely players perform each cut and screen, the harder the defense must work to keep up with the flurry of motion. Eventually, they'll miss an assignment, leaving someone open, and the offense can capitalize.

TOGETHER

Jeff Walz

Objective

To create an open look for the guard at the top of the key, or at least create a mismatch to catch an opponent's guard coming through screens late.

When to Use

When you need a quick bucket.

Key Personnel

The 2 should be a sharp shooter. The 3 should be able to shoot or drive and also to post if the variation is run. The posts are role players, but setting solid screens is crucial. 1 needs good passing skills and good timing; she must also be able to read the defense and know whether 3 will pop, curl, or flare off the double screen.

Execution

1 dribbles the ball to the right wing as 3 screens across for 2. If 2's defender slacks off at the screen, 2 should be open for 3 in the corner. Meanwhile, 3 uses a double screen from 4 and 5 to pop to the top of the key. 4 slips to the block (see the figure).

Variation

If the defense picks up on the play, 3 fakes the screen and rolls back with open hands, calling for the ball, while 2 fakes the cut to the corner and then comes off the double screen at the top. This still gets a player to the top of the key while potentially causing chaos within the defense.

Points of Emphasis

It's critical to set good screens and then to make hard cuts off the screens. If players are only going through the motions, defenders won't bite. They must make defenders believe the play is designed specifically for them.

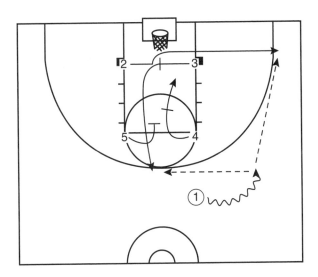

POST

Jeff Walz

Objective

To isolate a post against man-to-man or zone defense.

When to Use

- To capitalize on a post's size advantage.
- To get a quick bucket.
- To create a mismatch if the opponent is switching post-to-guard screens.
- Against a zone defense because the guards popping out is a good way to spread the zone and create openings.

Key Personnel

The 5 player should have a variety of post moves and be a go-to scorer down low. The 2 should be an effective catch-and-shooter who can also drive to the hoop. The 4 should have a decent midrange jumper or the ability to drive from the high post.

Execution

1. 1 dribbles to the right wing. 5 screens down for 2 as 4 screens down for 3 (figure 1).
2. 4 cuts hard to the ball-side elbow. 1 is looking for 5 posting hard on the block, for 4 flashing high, or for 2 at the top of the key (figure 2).

Variations

- The main objective is to score quickly in the post. However, if the opponent stays down to help, 3 might have a good opportunity to score coming off the screen.
- If 4's defender helps on the pick or with 5 posting, 4 might be able to flash to the middle of the lane for the pass.
- If a zone defense has seen the play a few times and begins to focus on 5 low or 1 and 2 high, 3 can flash to the middle of the lane for a short jumper.

Points of Emphasis

Without hard cuts, most quality opponents will not bite. If 2 doesn't cut up through the lane hard, calling for the ball, the defense might not be concerned with her and focus on 5. On the variations, the cutting players must catch their opponents off-guard by flashing quickly to the middle of the lane. In these cases, it's important to have a point guard at the top of her game who can react quickly to players adjusting to the defense.

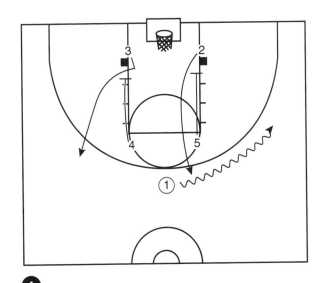

1

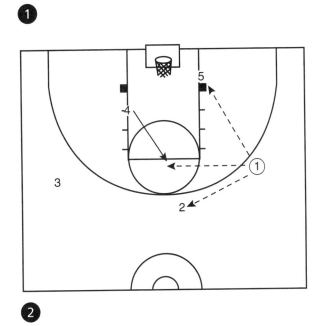

2

POINT DROP

Jeff Walz

Objective

To set a ball screen for the off-guard so she can attack or kick out to the point guard coming off a double screen.

When to Use

- When defenders are switching on ball screens, creating a mismatch.
- When a defense becomes complacent about communicating and fighting through and helping on screens.

Key Personnel

The point guard should have a good perimeter game, including the ability to knock down an open three. The 2 player should be able to drive and pull up in the lane as needed. The 3 and 5 players are used more as role players, but the 3 should be able to knock down the three-shot or a jumper from the baseline. The 4 should be proficient at the pick-and-roll.

Execution

1. 1 passes to 2 and then cuts to block off a screen from 4. 3 and 5 drop to get into position to set a double screen (figure 1).
2. As 2 dribbles off a ball screen by 4, 1 uses a double screen by 3 and 5 to get to the opposite wing, with 3 popping out to the corner and 5 posting up (figure 2).
3. 2 looks to attack while 4 rolls to the block looking for a pass (figure 3).

Variations

- A variation depends on the play of the opposing point guard. At times, after a pass, the defense will become complacent. In this case, a give-and-go could open up between 1 and 2 after the initial pass. 1 could also fake going off the double screen and roll back to post her defender.
- After 2 comes off the screen, the defense might try to hedge and help, so if the post pops out and switches, she'll have a good seal on the roll.

Points of Emphasis

Players sometimes lack the intensity to follow through with a play and execute it, especially if the play wasn't originally designed for them. This could be one of those plays, but with solid screens, hard cuts, and crisp passes, almost anyone on the court could wind up with an open look at the basket.

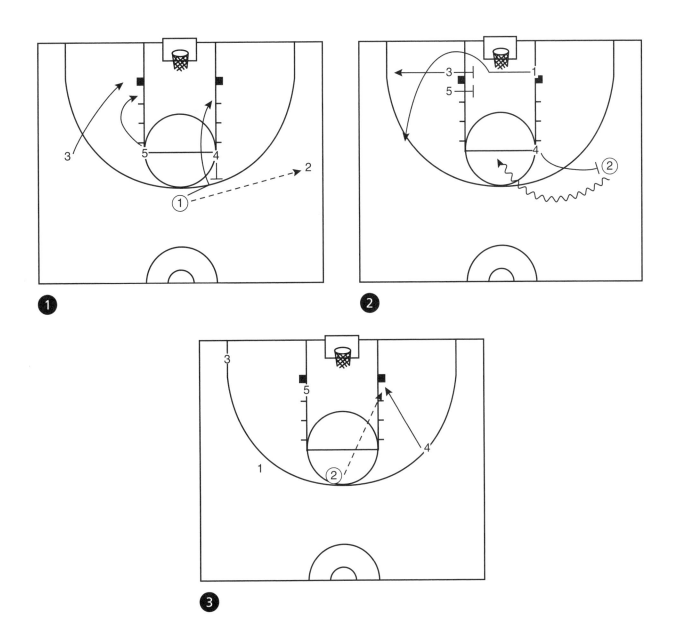

S

Jeff Walz

Objective

To get a guard open by weaving through the posts, causing her defender to chase.

When to Use

- Against a heavy-pressure man-to-man defense.
- When a guard is unable to get free from a tight defense.
- When a star player needs a good look.

Key Personnel

The 3 player must be able to catch and shoot or have the ability and quickness to penetrate to the rim. Posts must set good screens. The 4 should have a nice jumper from the foul line. The 5 needs a strong inside game.

Execution

1. 2 cuts to the opposite corner; 3 cuts across the high post to the opposite wing (figure 1).
2. 1 passes to 3; 4 sets a cross-screen for 5, who cuts to the ball-side block; 2 moves up to the wing (figure 2).
3. 3 looks to hit 4 at the high post or 5 posting hard on the block (figure 3).

Variation

If 3's defender is small, 1 can dribble to the right wing as 3 aborts her weave in the lane and posts up on the opposite block.

Points of Emphasis

All screens must be solid and all cuts hard. For instance, 2 and 3 must time their deliberate, hard cuts so that 1 doesn't handle the ball longer than necessary. 4 and 5 must set good screens, and 3 must use them well so she can lose her defender.

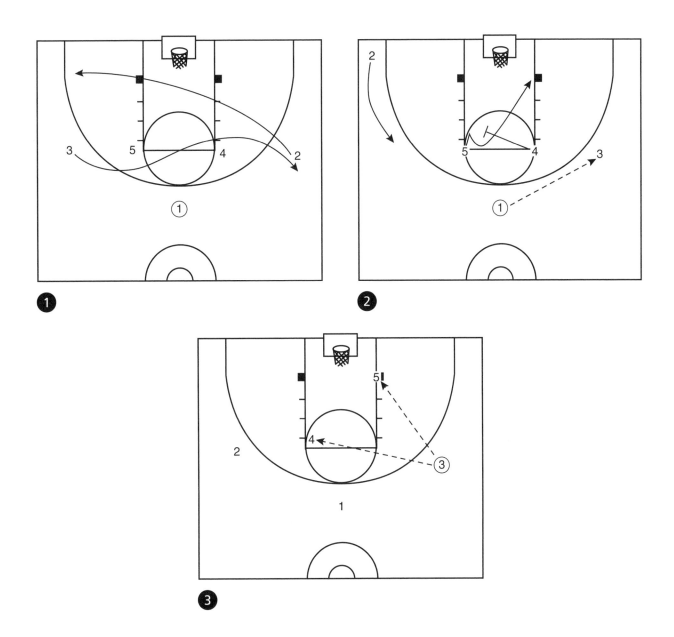

ELBOW

Gary Blair

Objectives
- To use specific cuts and scoring opportunities before moving into a motion offense.
- To give a power forward a one-on-one opportunity.

When to Use
- Against a man-to-man defense that does not switch on screens.
- When you have a power forward with enough athleticism to put the ball on the floor from the high-post position and take it to the hole.

Key Personnel
Your 4 needs a viable midrange game so that her defender must guard her at the elbow, but she must also have the ability to get to the basket with a variety of moves. The 1 must be strong and smart enough to angle her screen to make a larger defender struggle to get through it.

Execution
1. 1 passes the ball to 4 at the left elbow. Once 4 has caught the ball, 5 cuts from the right elbow to the left block to post up while 1 flashes to the middle of the paint as if she's cutting through to the baseline, but she then pivots back toward 4 to set a ball screen. After 1 gets her feet set, 4 sweeps through looking to penetrate to the basket. 2 and 3 remain high and wide on the wings (figure 1).
2. If 4 can't get to the basket, she passes to 3 before immediately posting up on the right block (figure 2).
3. When 3 receives the ball, a weave begins. 3 dribbles to the left elbow, looking to penetrate or to pull up for the midrange jumper, as 1 replaces 3 on the right wing (figure 3).
4. If 3 doesn't shoot, she passes to 2, who dribbles to the right elbow from the left wing, looking to penetrate or pull up for the midrange jumper. 3 replaces 2 on the left wing, and so the play continues until a shot is taken. Each time a guard penetrates toward a post, the post should work for position and ask for the ball (figure 4).

Variations
- Instead of screening for 4, 1 cuts through the paint toward the baseline and then out to replace 3 on the left wing. Immediately after 4 receives the ball, 3 cuts over the top of 4 for the handoff, looking to penetrate to the basket. 2 remains high and wide on the right wing (figure 5).
- If no shot is taken, 3 passes to 2 while 4 cuts to the right block to post up (figure 6). 2 dribbles to the left elbow, looking to penetrate or shoot the midrange jumper, and the weave continues.

Points of Emphasis
The two key players on the floor during this play are 1 and 4. This pre-motion offensive set is designed to give 4 an opportunity to go one on one to the basket. The timing of 1's screen for 4 is critical because 1 must have her feet and angle set before 4 faces up and makes a move. If 4 goes too soon, 1 could be called for a moving screen. Patience on the pass, the ball screen, and the drive is important so that no silly fouls are called. 5 must shield off her defender while 4 drives, and the guards should always be in triple-threat position.

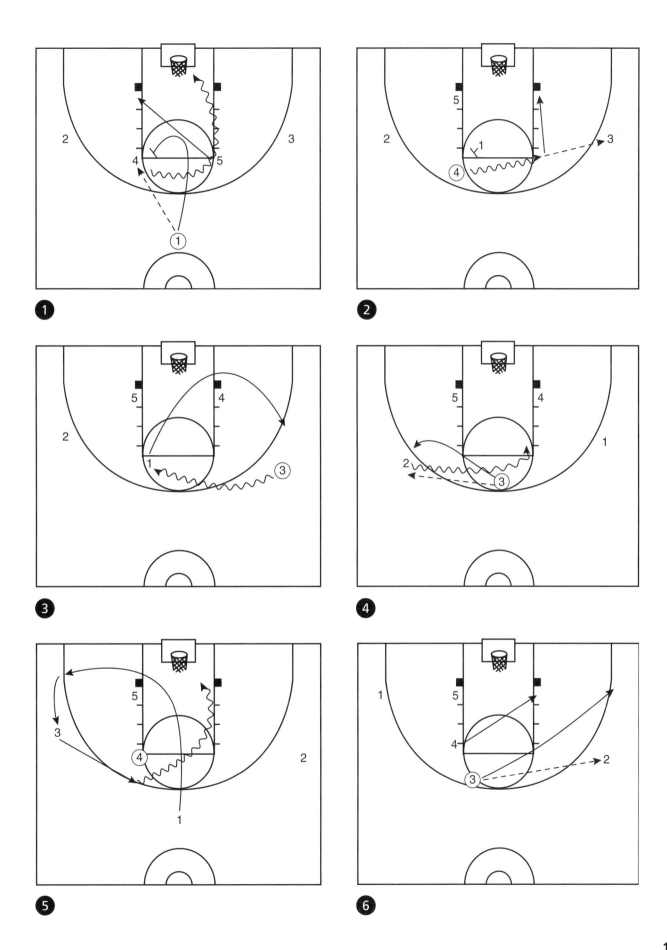

EXCHANGE

Gary Blair

Objectives

- To isolate both post players while they work together to create a one-on-one move in the paint.
- To create an opportunity for the point guard to penetrate to the basket for an easy layup.

When to Use

Against an opponent mismatched in the low post when the defense switches on the post-to-post down screen.

Key Personnel

Your 1 must have the ball-handling skills to go full speed off the screen but to be able to stop and shoot a midrange jumper if her defense goes under the screen. The 4 and 5 must work well together on screens and passes, knowing each other's strengths and weaknesses while reading the defense.

Execution

1. Starting near the left sideline, 1 dribbles off 5's high-low screen at the top of the key and looks to penetrate to the basket or pull up for the midrange jump shot. If the defense switches, 5 should immediately spin, pin her smaller defender, and ask for a direct pass from 1. 2 drops to the right corner (figure 1).

2. If 1 does not take a shot, she continues dribbling to the right wing. 5 immediately sets a down screen for 4 on the left block. 4 cuts to the left elbow or to the arc if comfortable shooting the three. 5 rolls to pin her defender, looking for the direct pass from 1 (figure 2).

3. If the pass isn't there, 1 passes to 4, who looks for 5 in a one-on-one situation. 5 rolls to pin her defender (figure 3).

Variation

Anytime the offense does not attempt a shot from a high-low offense set, the point guard should call her teammates into a motion offense to create movement via cuts and screens. Because there are limited options off a high-low set, motion helps create a diversion for the defense while keeping them honest.

Points of Emphasis

Post players focus on learning to work together, reading what the other does for positioning purposes. It's also essential for the point guard to understand that the first option is to penetrate to the basket. Timing for this play is critical. The 5 should never down-screen for 4 until after 1 has cleared the on-ball screen to keep the lane clear.

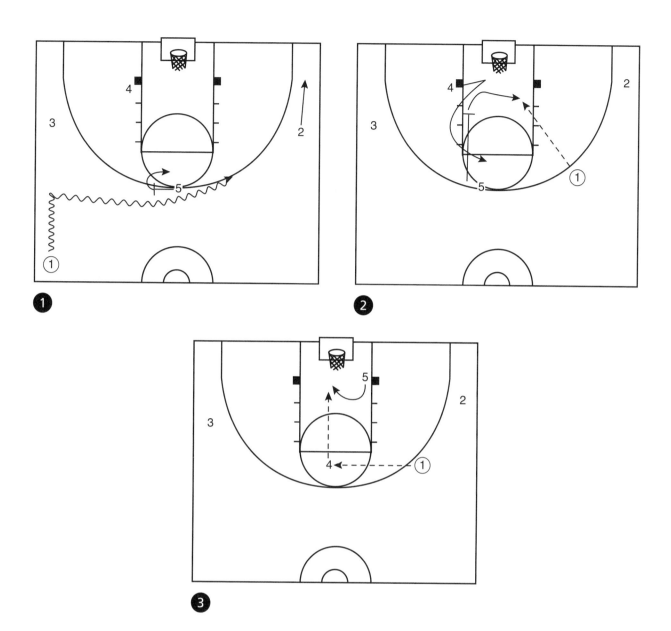

OVERLOAD HIGH

Gary Blair

Objectives

- To overload one side of the court while letting the low post work for the backside pin position.
- To free up a shooter if there's no advantage gained in the post.
- To exploit the lack of true backside help.

When to Use

Against a man-to-man defense that likes to play in the passing lanes, deny all positions, and front the low post.

Key Personnel

The 1 and 5 are the key offensive positions in this play. The 1 must be able to make an effective lob pass that won't get deflected by a defender denying on the front side, especially if 1 gives up height to her defender. The 5 should be a dominant player effective one on one. The 2 should be a good shooter from the corner.

Execution

1 dribble-entries to the right wing, pushing 2 to the corner. At the same time, 3 cuts from the left wing to about 6 to 8 feet (1.8-2.4 m) above the three-point line for spacing purposes, while 4 cuts from the left block to the right elbow. 5 should be working to pin her defender on the back side with her chest facing the baseline and her back facing the middle of the paint. 1 makes a high lob pass to 5 for a short jumper (figure 1).

Variations

- If the defense opts to zone off each player and take away the lob pass to the low post, 1 reverses the ball to 3 at the top of the key instead of passing to 5 to use the vacant left side of the court (figure 2). The 3 dribbles to the left wing to continue reversing the ball, as 4 rolls to the opposite low block to set a stagger screen with 5. The 2 uses the screens to cut through the baseline to the opposite corner (figure 3).
- The 1 might be able to hit 4 on the elbow instead of passing to 5 or 2. The 4's first option then would be to feed 5 on the right block. Her second option is to penetrate to the basket using a left-handed dribble.

Points of Emphasis

This play seems fairly simple but can be very hard to guard. Patience and reversing the ball are important to keep the defense moving and a new defender deciding whether to help with backside post defense or to defend her player to the three-point line. Timing is also important. Players don't begin their move to the strong side, and 5 shouldn't start working for the backside pin, until 1 begins her dribble to the right wing.

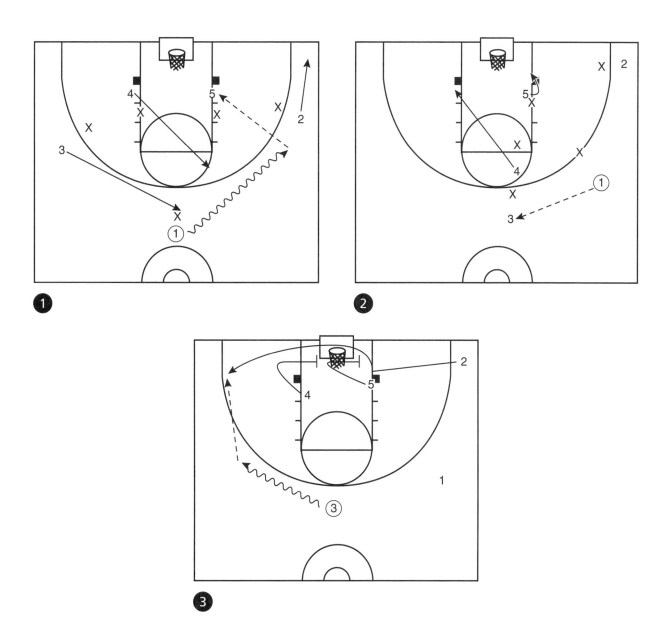

X-DOUBLE

Gary Blair

Objective

To create a quick shot while getting the offense into a motion set.

When to Use

- Against a man-to-man defense mismatched at the guard positions.
- To create a last-second shot or to run down the shot clock.

Key Personnel

Your 3 should be a big, combination player with ability to post up and make a one-on-one move at the low-post position. It's advantageous if the 4 can step out and hit the three. Post players must set proper screens and understand the techniques of a motion set.

Execution

1. 1 dribbles to the left wing, sending 2 through the baseline to the right short corner. 3 cuts between 4 and 5 at each elbow position to the left-side block, looking for the post-up (figure 1).

2. If 3 does not immediately get the ball inside, 4 and 5 set a staggered down-screen for 2. 1 passes to 2 for a three-point shot (figure 2).

3. If 2 does not take the three, 4 spins to the outside and sets a ball screen for 2 looking for the midrange jump shot while 5 posts up on the right block asking for the ball (figure 3).

4. Once 4 screens, she pops back to the three-point line to create a four-out, one-in motion set (figure 4).

Points of Emphasis

Although the play seems quite simple, it's very important for players to understand the disadvantage of not attacking the basket. Ball and player movement is important because it forces the defense to work to keep up with the frequent cuts made off screens. The 3 is easily the most important player on the court. If she can attract the attention of the post players' defense, this frees up the 2, who's looking for an outside shot. Once the play has been run through its entirety and the quick-hit isn't available, the play becomes a motion set—the best of both worlds.

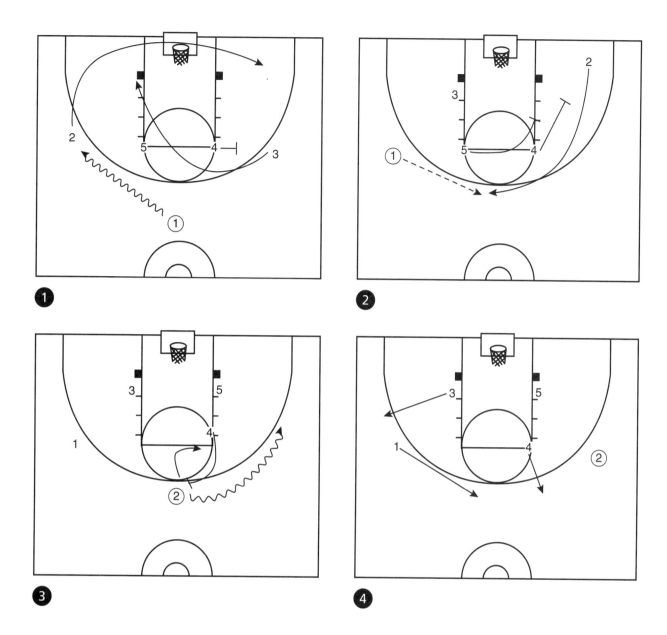

DOUBLE HIGH STACK

Gary Blair

Objectives

- To post up a player with a size advantage over her defender and create an open three-pointer for a guard.
- To keep the defense honest and in check.
- To get every position on the court involved.

When to Use

- If your team thrives in motion sets.
- When you don't have dominant post players in the game but do have aggressive guards.
- Against a man-to-man defense that tries to battle through screens without switching.

Key Personnel

The best scenario of players is two combination guards and post players who are versatile enough to shoot the three. The play works well with a smaller lineup. A dominant 5 is not as important as a 3 who has the size and physicality to post up a smaller guard. The 2 must be a shooter who comes off a stagger screen with her feet set and ready to shoot.

Execution

1. 4 pops out to the right wing. 1 passes to 4 and then immediately down-screens for 5 at the left elbow. 5 cuts to the top of the key while 2 sets a cross-screen in the middle of the paint for 3. 3 comes over the top of the screen and posts up on the right block, asking for the pass from 4 (figure 1).
2. If 3 does not receive the pass, 4 reverses the ball to 5, 1 pops out to the left wing, and 3 and 4 set a staggered down screen for 2. 5 passes to 2 for a jumper, if she curls the last screen, or a three-pointer if she uses a straight-line cut (figure 2).

Variation

If no shot is taken from the original options, the play can be extended. If 2 is not open off the stagger screen, 5 passes to 1 on the left wing, assuming the defense has switched all screens. 3 posts up momentarily on the left block and then cross-screens for 4 on the right block. 4 goes over the top of the screen to post up, looking for the short jumper. At the same time, 5 sets a down screen for 2 on the right wing to create motion in case 4 does not receive the pass (figure 3).

Points of Emphasis

The basic fundamentals of basketball are key to the success of this play, but none more than the timing and setting up of the screens. Also, 4 should focus on getting her body set in triple-threat position so the defense has no other option but to respect her ability to shoot, drive, or pass. The 3 must know how to come off a low-post-to-low-post screen and understand how to use her body to post up.

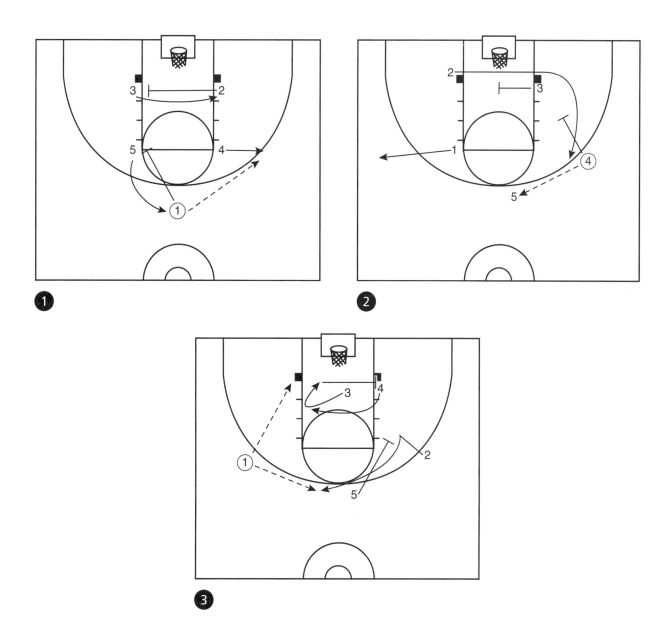

BALL SCREEN

Lisa Stone

Objective

To use ball screens and ball reversals to stretch a defense and open up scoring opportunities.

When to Use

- Against a team playing man-to-man defense that struggles with ball-screen defense.
- In some cases, against a 2-3 zone.
- In a quick-hit situation.
- As a new look in transitioning into a motion offense.

Key Personnel

The 2 must read the defense, get deep into the paint with her dribble, and work well with a versatile post player. The 5 must create off the bounce or hit a 15-footer. The 1 must be a solid outside shooter.

Execution

1. 1 dribbles into position, passes to 2, and then cuts through to the strong-side corner (figure 1).
2. 5 sets a ball screen so 2 can attack the middle of the paint from the high side. If 2 doesn't have a shot, she passes to 5 either rolling down or stepping high or reverses to 3. 2 then cuts to the strong-side corner (figure 2).
3. If 3 receives the ball, 4 sets a ball screen so 3 can attack the middle of the paint from the high side. Like 2 before, 3 looks for a shot in the lane, works with 4 rolling down or stepping high, or kicks it down to 2 or over to 1 (figure 3).

Variation

The play can be run in either direction. Dribble-pushing the guard on the wing to the corner is an option if the defense denies the wing pass. The opposite post (in this case 4) could set the initial screen, which provides the guard more room for dribble penetration.

Points of Emphasis

Maintaining spacing and using the ball screens are most important. Patient and explosive guards who read the defense well can create great scoring opportunities for themselves or the posts. The post might have to slip the screen if the defense provides a high and very hard hedge on the screen. Beware of defenses that trap ball screens. If they do, and if the guard lacks good vision out of the double team, a turnover is likely. Inconsistent three-point shooters will allow defenses to sag in and protect the basket.

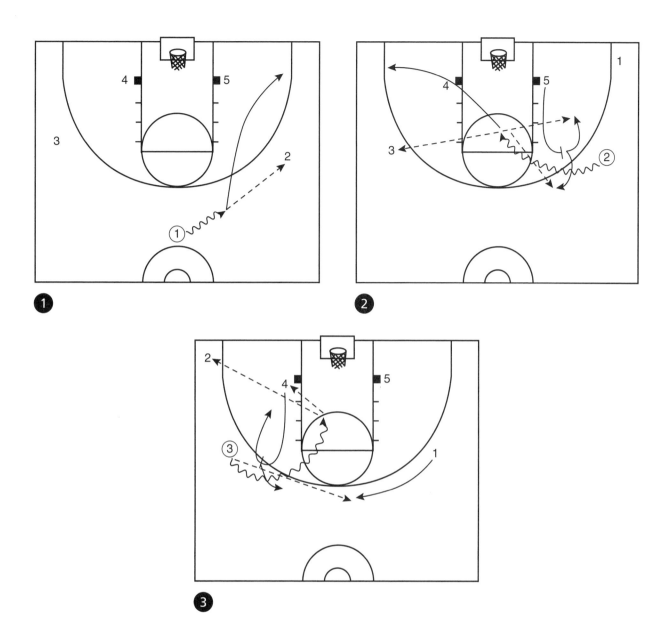

5

Post Plays vs. Zone Defense

Nearly every team will play both man-to-man and zone defense, depending on their opponent. Not only will matchups pose problems for a team executing a certain defense against certain opponents, but mixing up the look and style of an offense can take an opponent out of its comfort zone and flow. Thus every offense should have plays designed to attack a zone defense in addition to man to man.

Man-to-man offenses create openings via player and ball movement and by using screens. Zone offenses create openings by attacking weak spots in the defense—and every zone has them. Because zone defenders are focused first on a specific area instead of a specific player, the weaknesses in a zone are the places where defenders are not positioned, such as at the baseline and high wing in a 1-3-1; the middle, wing, and high wing in a 1-2-2; and the top of the key, wings, and between the blocks in a 2-1-2.

Zone offenses still rely on player and ball movement and some screens, but the movements must be made with the zone alignment and defender assignments in mind. Zones require more precise movement because defenders are covering specific areas rather than defending particular players wherever they go. Understanding the initial alignment and subsequent seams based on player and ball movement allows an offense to devise ways to find gaps and make something happen.

Perimeter players might take a cursory look at a zone, see no openings, and take an outside shot. Although this works at times, living by the outside shot is seldom your best game plan. An offense wants to take as many high-percentage shots as possible, which in most cases are shots closest to the rim. Some of the plays in this chapter offer an outlet or option for an outside shot, and some call for the post to have the range to shoot a 15-foot jumper or even a three-point shot, but the primary objective is to get post players touches inside by isolating them on the block, creating a two-person game between the best shooter and low-post player, stretching the zone, and overloading one side of the court.

Post players must have the size and skills to execute inside plays. Perimeter players must have the skills to help create openings and get the ball inside. Posts should be very active and able to read the defense, flash to an area into which the ball can be delivered, gain position on and hold their own against defenders, finish shots in traffic, and cover the weak-side offensive boards. For some plays, they also need to be able to shoot the midrange (or even long-range) jumper, create shots for teammates, and set and read screens. Guards will need to be active, read the defense, make good passes, set good screens, slash to the rim, and threaten to score from the outside.

All players need to understand the general principles of attacking a zone. Players and the ball must move frequently and quickly to make the defense work harder. Players drive or slash to the openings between defenders, which often leads to two defenders guarding one player, thus leaving another player open. Try to overload one side of the court. Employ pass fakes as well as reverse, skip, and diagonal passes, though not necessarily on the first or second rotation.

2 GUARD

Rick Insell

Objective

To get an open look at the basket from either the three-point line on the wing or in the paint.

When to Use

When faced with a standard 1-3-1 half-court zone defense, with normal shifts and movements, but not against a matchup zone.

Key Personnel

Put your four best three-point shooters on the floor, with the best shooter at the 4 spot. The 5 should be a very mobile and athletic player.

Execution

1 passes to 4 in the corner. 5 dives to the block, posts up, and looks for the ball. If 5 is not open, 1 passes to 2 while 5 flashes high. 2 passes the ball to 3, and 5 dives again ball side (see the figure).

Points of Emphasis

Alignment is critical to this play. The four perimeter players should have equal distance between them and stay deep and wide, ready to shoot immediately upon receiving the ball or to progress the ball into the slots or the three-point line. 1 and 2 should split the top of the 1-3-1 and *always* look to 5 flashing high. Even a fake pass will shift the defense enough to get an open shot in the corner. 5 should be very active throughout the play and look to the rim first when she receives the ball. Players move the ball corner to corner quickly to make the entire zone move and the baseline defender run as much as possible. Avoid diagonal or skip passes on the first rotation. Eventually, the skip will be open, but only after the ball has touched all four perimeter players' hands.

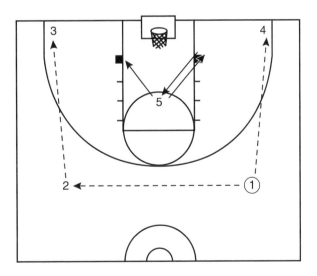

GOLD

Kathy Miller

Objectives

- To isolate the best low-post player one on one on the block.
- To get a layup for the most aggressive perimeter player.
- To get an open perimeter jump shot for the point guard.
- To make the opponent defend a second stagger screen and create a scoring opportunity for the best wing player.

When to Use

- As a secondary break in transition or in the half-court set.
- When the post players are secondary scorers.

Key Personnel

The post players should be strong, tough screeners because that's their primary role in this play, although the 4 player should be able to knock down an open jumper and pass well in the low post. The 2 should be good at slashing to the rim off a back screen and adept at reading and coming off a stagger screen to knock down a shot. The 1 should have the ability to come off the stagger screen and either knock down the jumper at the top of the key or hit the cutter coming off the screen.

Execution

1. 1 brings the ball up on the right side, passes to 2 on the wing, and cuts to the strong-side corner while 3 occupies her defender by taking her low to the corner and then back to the wing (figure 1).

2. 2 reverses the ball through 4 to 3 on the left wing. 5 sets a back screen for 2, who heads to the strong-side block, looking for a pass from 2 (figure 2).

3. 5 immediately heads to the corner to set the first stagger screen for 1, with 4 following suit, so 1 can move to the top of the arc. 3 hits 1, who shoots the jumper if she's open (figure 3).

4. If 1 doesn't have a shot, 5 and 4 set a stagger screen for 2, who heads to the right baseline or wing. 5's screen should be in the middle of the key under rim, and 4's screen should be on the right-side block. Depending on how 2's defender plays, 2 will look to flare or curl (figure 4).

Points of Emphasis

3 must time her cut to get open on the reverse. As the second player in the first stagger screen, 4 needs to read how 1's defender is playing and set the screen in the area in which it will be most effective. 1 must read how her defender is playing the stagger and be prepared to straight cut, curl, fade, or backdoor to get open. If she doesn't shoot, she needs to dribble toward 2 to shorten the pass. As 1 did, 2 reads her defender off the second stagger screen, looking to curl or dribble into the lane to look for a shot.

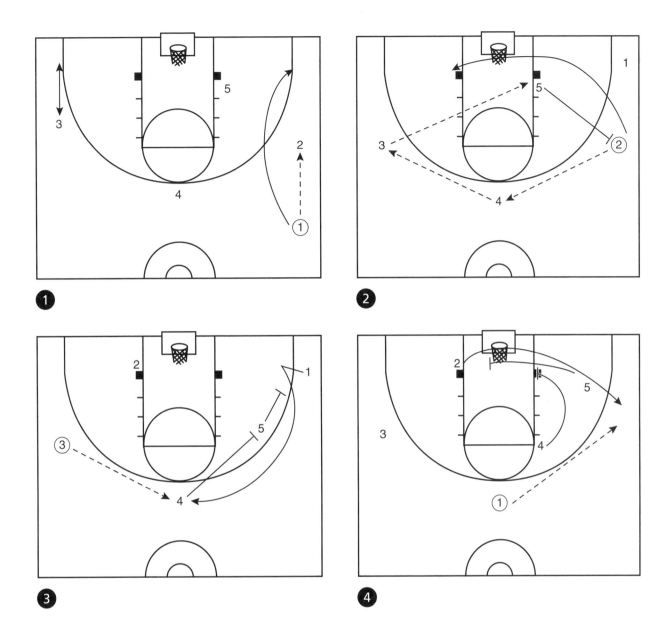

SLICE

Kathy Miller

Objectives

- To isolate the best low-post player one on one on the block.
- To create a two-man game between the best shooter and the low-post player.
- To create an open jump shot for the best post player who can knock down the three-point shot.
- To take advantage of a low-post defender who doesn't want to guard on the perimeter.

When to Use

- At any time during a game.
- At the end of a game to get the ball in the best low-post player's hands on the block.

Key Personnel

The 5 player must be a very good one-on-one low-post player—ideally, a player the opponent must double-team. The 4 should be able to knock down a three to keep her defender honest. The 3 should be a very good screener and the best perimeter shooter. The 2 must be able to shoot the ball to stretch the defense, allowing the 5 to work one on one on the block.

Execution

1. 3 down-screens on the opposite block for 4, who cuts to the left wing, while 2 pops to the right wing. 1 passes the ball to 4 (figure 1).
2. 5 takes a step inside the key and screens for 3, who breaks to the left corner. 4 looks inside to 5. If she's not open, she passes to 3, who looks for a shot (figure 2).
3. If 3 doesn't shoot, she looks inside for 5. If 5's defender is playing behind, 3 passes inside to 5. If 5's defender is playing in front, 3 skips the ball to 2 on the right wing, who hits 5 sealing off her defender (figure 3).

Points of Emphasis

The 3 must hunt 4's defender and set the screen on the midline. 4 then cuts over the top of 3's screen, forcing her defender to trail the play. As soon as 3 has set the screen, she cuts underneath 5 and goes to the ball-side corner. 1 delivers the ball where 4 can shoot it. 4's reads are, in order: shoot, feed 5 at the low post, or kick to 3 in the ball-side corner for a shot.

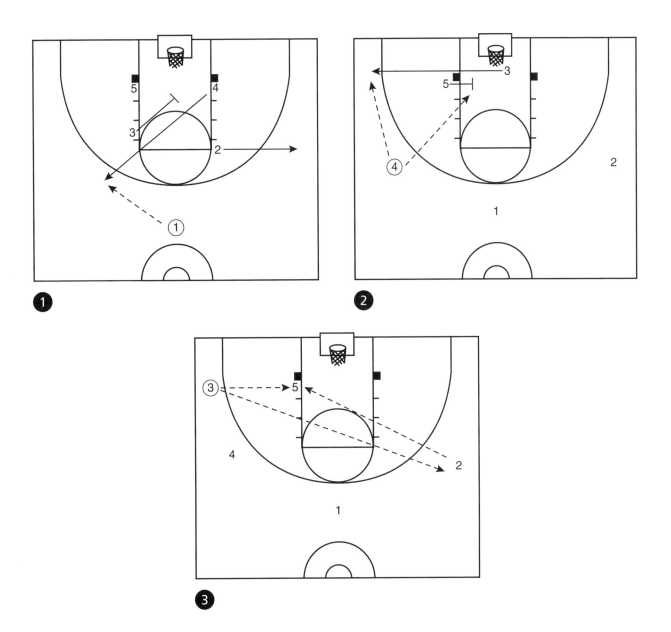

2 DOWN

MaChelle Joseph

Objective

To get an easy corner jumper for the post player.

When to Use

- Against almost any type of zone defense.
- As a quick-hit zone offense.

Key Personnel

The post player must be capable of setting good screens. At least one very good shooter needs to be on the floor to keep the defense honest so they don't clog the middle of the paint.

Execution

1. 1 passes to 2 on the right wing, just to let her touch the ball. 2 passes right back to 1, who reverses the ball to 3 (figure 1).

2. 2 runs the baseline, going through to the opposite corner and running off a screen that 5 sets on the outside defender of the zone. Meanwhile, 3 penetrates to the free-throw line and passes to 1 (figure 2).

3. 1 skips the ball to 2 in the corner, who shoots if she's open. Otherwise she passes to 4, who's curling off 5's screen in the middle of the zone defense for a short jumper (figure 3).

Points of Emphasis

Timing is important. When the ball is reversed to 3 on the left wing, she needs to penetrate as soon as she gets the ball while 2 is running the baseline so that 2 is not waiting too long in the corner for the skip pass. Also, 5 should not set the screen on the middle person of the zone defense until 2 has the ball. When first running this play, 2 will be wide open in the corner for the three. After the play has been run a few times, 4 should have a wide-open jumper.

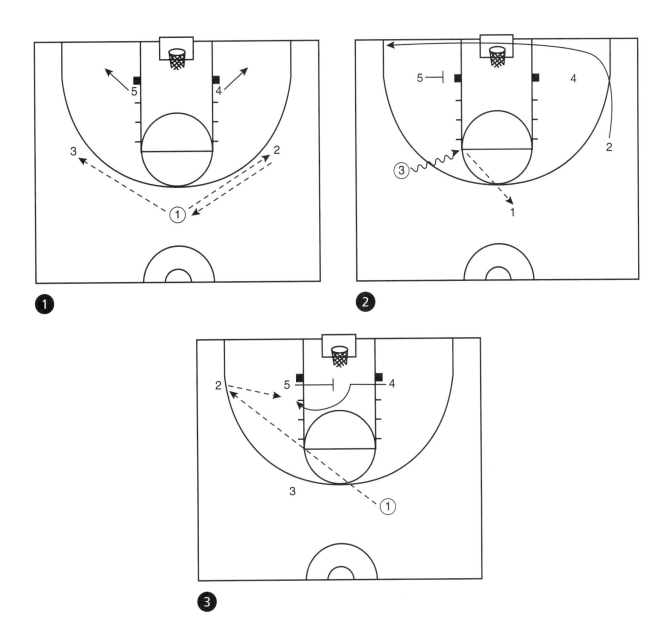

MAC

MaChelle Joseph

Objectives

- To get a layup for the post player.
- To get a three-point shot from the corner.

When to Use

Best against a 3-2 or 2-3 zone defense, but works against most zones because the screening on the baseline breaks down formations.

Key Personnel

To run this play effectively, you need a post player capable of screening and pinning her defender as well as scoring with physical contact. At least one shooter should also be on the floor so the defense can't clog the middle of the paint.

Execution

1. 1 passes to 2 on the right wing. 4, who is the trailer, flashes to the high-post elbow on ball side. The ball is then reversed from 2 to 1 to 3 while 4 dives to the low block and 5 flashes to the elbow (figure 1).

2. 3 dribbles to the lane line extended to pull her defender away from the action while 4 steps out to the short corner and 5 dives to the ball-side low block. 1 shifts right for spacing, and 2 drops to the corner (figure 2).

3. 3 passes to 1 and then sprints to the weak-side corner. 5 sets a screen for 4 coming across the lane and then pins and seals her defender. 1 attacks the free-throw line, looking to lob to 5 or to feed 3 for the three (figure 3).

4. If these two options are not available, 1 passes to 2 on the wing, 5 flashes to the elbow, and the play continues (figure 4).

Variation

If the lob pass to 5 is not open, 5 sets a screen for 3 in the corner for the three-pointer.

Points of Emphasis

Timing and post positioning are very important. Neither 2 nor 3 with the ball on the wing can dribble to pull her defender away from the action unless there are posts on the low block and elbow. The post can't step out to the short corner and dive to the low block until 2 or 3 dribbles to pull the defense away, and 5 must wait on the pass to 1 to set the screen for 4. The play is effective because at some point four offensive players are along the baseline and the defense has a very difficult time matching all of them, leaving someone with an open shot.

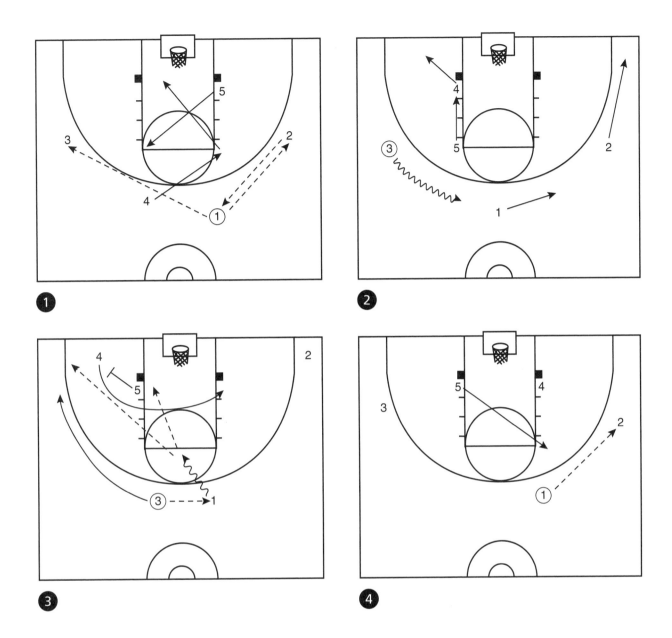

OOP

MaChelle Joseph

Objective

To get a quick layup on the back side of the zone.

When to Use

- Against any type of zone defense.
- As a quick-hit zone offense.

Key Personnel

The 1 player needs to pass the ball well; the 4 should be very good at setting screens.

Execution

1. 1 passes to 2 on the right wing and then switches places with 3 (figure 1).
2. 2 reverses the ball to 3, who passes to 1. During the reversal, 5 follows the ball to the opposite low block (figure 2).
3. 4 sets a back screen on the back side of the zone for 2, who flashes in for an alley-oop pass from 1 (figure 3).
4. If the pass is not there, 2 continues running through to the opposite side, 1 dribbles to the top of the key, 3 replaces 2 on the right wing, and the play continues on the left side (figure 4).

Points of Emphasis

The 5 player must be very active and call for the ball while following it to the opposite low block. Most important, 4 must set a very good screen on the back side of the zone defense to allow 2 a clear path to the basket.

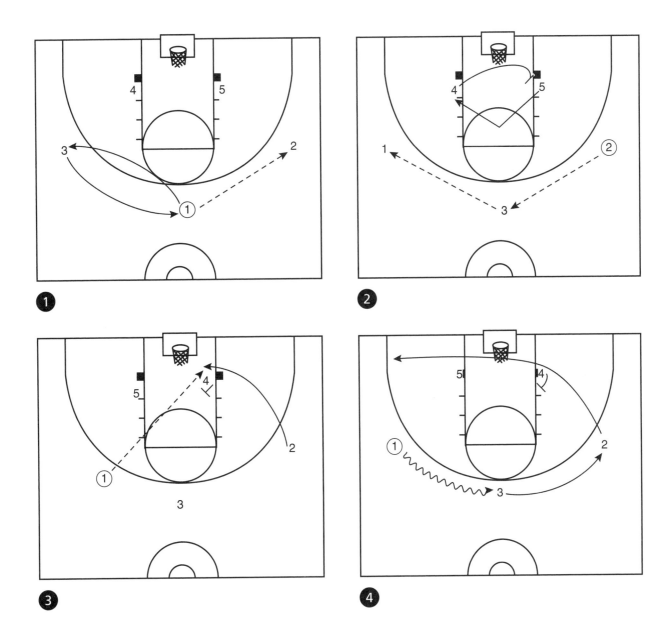

STAY

MaChelle Joseph

Objective

To get an easy jump shot from the free-throw area or penetration to the basket by the power forward.

When to Use

- Against almost any type of zone defense.
- As a quick hit or continuous zone offense.

Key Personnel

The 4 player must be very active and capable of scoring from the high post via a jumper or off penetration. She must also be able to create shots for teammates.

Execution

1. 1 passes to 3, who dribbles to the top of the key. 4 replaces 3 on the left wing, 2 replaces 4 at the free-throw line, and 1 replaces 2 on the right wing. 5 remains ball side on the low block (figure 1).

2. The shuffling process continues, either in the same order or reversed, until 4 is back at the high post (figure 2).

3. At any point the ball can go to 4 in the high-post area; she looks to shoot or hit 5 on the block. 2 and 3 sprint to the corners (figure 3).

Variation

Once 4 has scored from the high post a couple of times, she can kick the ball out to the guards in the corners for open three-point shots.

Point of Emphasis

The ball must get into the high-post area as much as possible to give 4 several options: scoring herself, hitting 5 posted up in the paint, or hitting 2 or 3 in the corners.

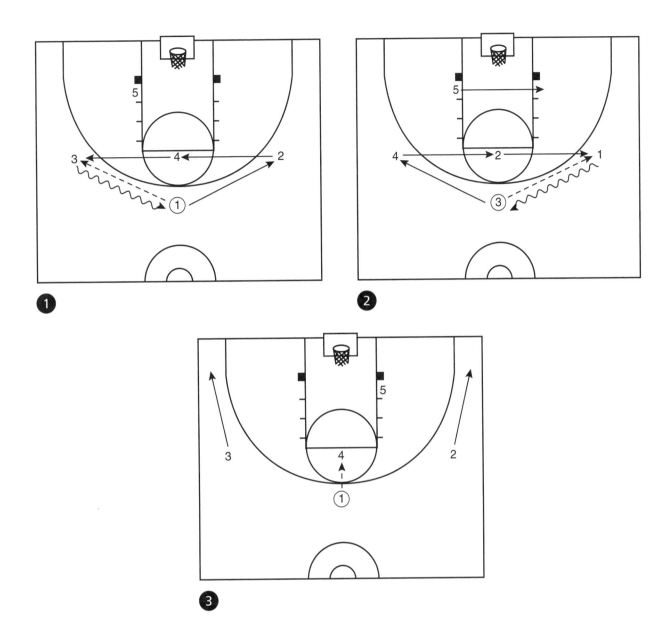

ZONE O

MaChelle Joseph

Objective

To stretch out the zone defense by overloading on the ball side.

When to Use

- Against any type of zone defense.
- As a quick-hit zone offense.
- As a continuous offense to run time off the clock.

Key Personnel

All five players must be able to set good screens, read the defense, and cut to open areas.

Execution

1. 1 dribbles to the right wing while 2 shallow-cuts and replaces 1 at the top of the key. 1 keeps her dribble alive (figure 1). A shallow cut loops from the wing back to the top of the key.

2. 3 comes from the opposite wing to set a screen for 1, and 2 replaces 3 on the left wing. 1 dribbles off the screen to the top of the key, while 3 spots up after the screen looking for the shot (figure 2).

3. 1 passes to 3. If the shot is not there, 4 steps out to the short corner looking for the ball, and 2 flashes into the high-post area, also looking for the ball. 5 replaces 4 on the ball-side block (figure 3).

4. If neither 2 nor 4 is open, 2 goes back out to the wing. 3 reverses the ball through 1 to the opposite wing after passing to 4 (figure 4).

5. Once the ball is reversed, 5 sets a screen on the zone defense for 4 to come across the lane to the opposite block for the pass and shot (figure 5).

Variation

Because 4 stretches out the defense by running to the short corner, the skip pass to the opposite guard will be available if she stays on the wing.

Point of Emphasis

The 4 player should at least touch the ball in the short corner area to open up a shot for 5 posted up in the paint for a layup or the opposite guard for a three-pointer.

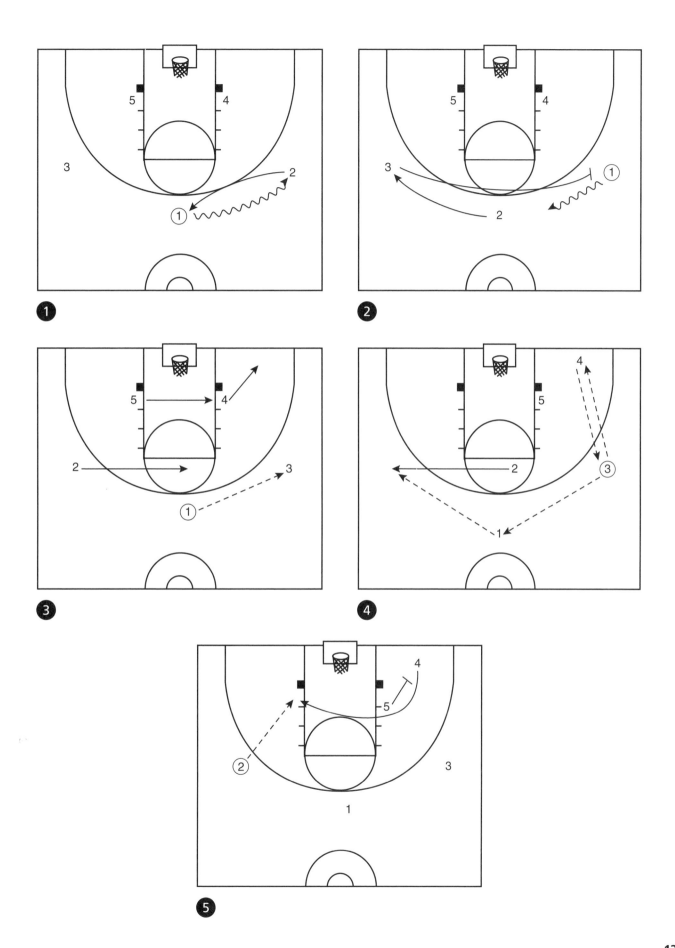

BASELINE

Rick Insell

Objective

To get an open look at the basket from either the three-point line on the wing or in the paint.

When to Use

When faced with a standard 2-3 half-court zone defense, with normal shifts and movements, but not against a matchup zone.

Key Personnel

The best three-point shooters should be in the game on the perimeter, with the hottest at the 2 spot. The 4 should be the most mobile and athletic player and the 5 a power finisher who changes directions well.

Execution

1. 1 passes to the wing on the side of whichever defender picks her up, in this case 2. 2 looks for a shot or a pass to 5, and 1 shifts toward 2. If 5 receives the ball, 4 dives to the front of the basket for a pass or to rebound on the weak side (figure 1).

2. If the pass isn't there, 2 reverses the ball back to 1 and then 3. 4 and 5 follow the ball with target hands (figure 2).

3. If 4 receives the ball in the high post, 5 slips inside to the basket for a high-low seal or to gain rebounding position (figure 3).

Variation

If the zone isn't guarding the player at the top of the key, move the best three-point shooter to the 1 slot. She will get the majority of the shots because the top two defenders are trying to cover all three perimeter players and cheating to get to the wings sooner.

Points of Emphasis

Alignment is critical to the execution of this play. The 1 player begins the play in the center of the zone to make a defender commit. 2 and 3 align themselves in the slot between the bottom and top defenders on their respective sides and stay in the direct center of these players to make it difficult for them to decide who to cover. 4 stays between the two hash marks closest to the foul line (but not *on* the foul line). This eliminates the top of the zone matching up with her. 5 aligns with her heels starting on the baseline and behind the backboard. 2 is often open after two reversals.

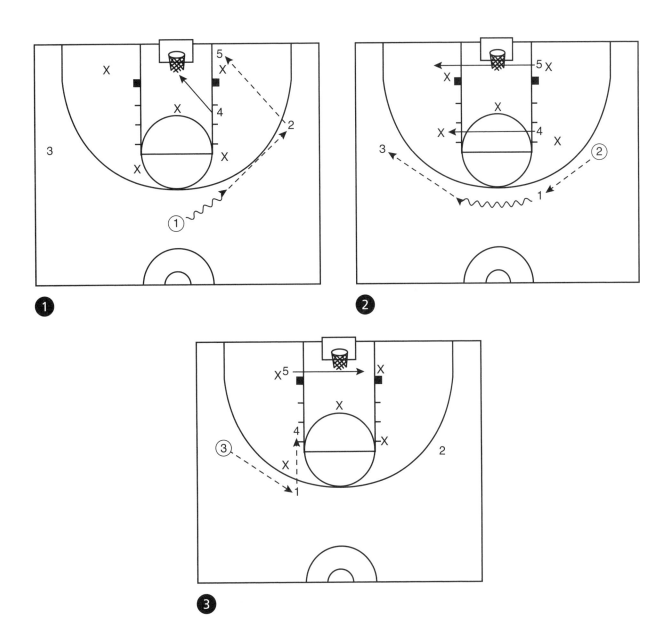

THREE

Rick Insell

Objective

To get an open look at the basket from either the three-point line on the wing or in the paint.

When to Use

- When facing a standard 2-3 half-court zone defense, with normal shifts and movements, but not a matchup zone.
- Against a man-to-man defense if players are active enough to use ball screens effectively.

Key Personnel

The 5 should be an effective three-point shooter and a good passer and decision maker.

Execution

1. 1 dribbles to the center of the zone to freeze the defense. When a defender picks her up, the wing on that side (in this case 5) sets a ball screen. 1 dribbles off the screen toward the sideline looking for a shot as 4 posts to the middle of the zone (figure 1).

2. If 1 doesn't have a shot, she passes to 5. 5 looks for a quick open shot or for 4 flashing high but then immediately reverses the ball to 2 if no one is open. 3 runs the baseline to the opposite corner, and 4 drops to the ball-side block (figure 2).

3. 5 sets a ball screen for 2, who dribbles to the center of the free-throw line and continues until she scores or a defender stops her. 1 spaces to the top of the key. If nothing is there, 2 kicks the ball out to 1, and the play continues (figure 3).

Points of Emphasis

On-ball screens must be solid and on a body. Allowing the defense to easily get over or under an open-space screen will quickly break down the offense. The screener should then space to the three-point line. 3 must be persistent, looking for her shot on all touches, and 4 must be active and offense-minded.

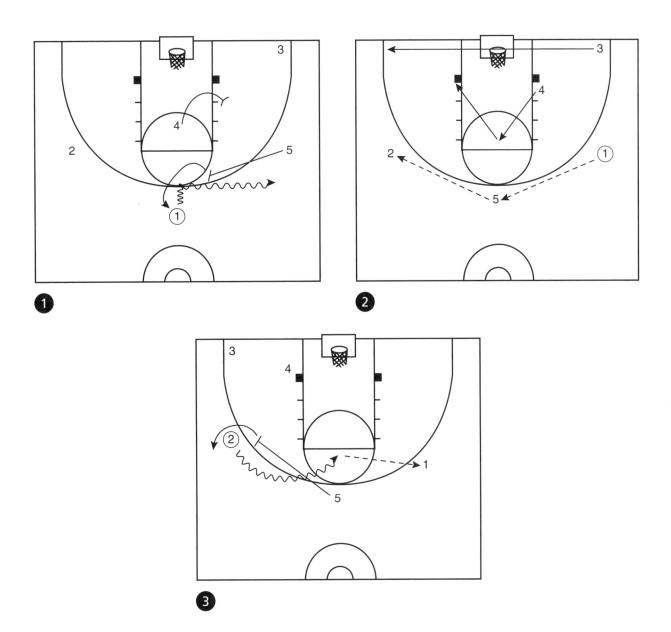

DRIBBLE MOTION

Rick Insell

Objective

To get an open look at the basket from either the three-point line on the wing or in the interior of the painted area.

When to Use

When faced with an odd front zone (1-2-2, 3-2, or 1-3-1) or a matchup zone of any kind.

Key Personnel

Your three best three-point shooters are on the perimeter. 3 must be active and able to catch and shoot. The post players have the same responsibilities—reading the open areas of the zone and finding the gaps when flashing to the ball—and thus are interchangeable.

Execution

1. 1 dribbles to the sideline on the side of the floor she wants to attack, in this case the right. 3 drops to the dead corner while 2 shifts over to be ready for the ball reversal. 4 takes about three steps up the lane, finds the gap in the zone, and then flashes to the ball with target hands. 5 posts up the defender closest to the basket (figure 1).

2. If nobody is open, 1 passes to 2, who drives hard to the opposite wing to make a defender commit to her. 1 shifts over to be ready for the ball reversal. At the same time, 3 runs the baseline to the other dead corner while 4 posts up the defender 5 has just posted up by whipping her leg around her defender. 5 flashes to the gap at the high post, and the play continues (figure 2).

Points of Emphasis

Players should remain spaced about 15 to 18 feet (4.5-5.4 m) apart at all times. 1 must get to the sideline quickly. This offense will not be effective from the center of the floor. On the ball reversal, the player at the top of the key must drive hard and look to score first to make the top of the zone commit. If 3 is persistent in running the baseline, she will get open looks. The post players cover the weak side for an offensive rebound, cutting diagonally if at the high post and rolling out to the opposite side if in the low post. They must also be aware of who to post up and where to flash. The worst thing a post player can do is flash into someone's back or to an area where the ball can't be delivered.

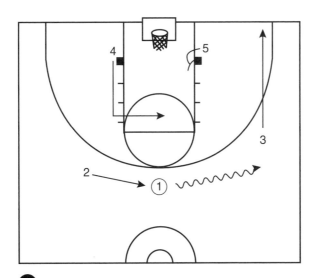

1

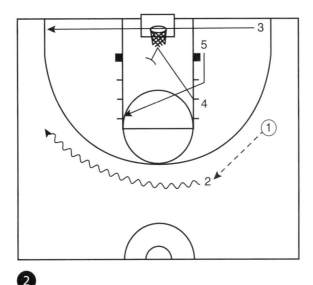

2

ZONE STACK

Rick Insell

Objective

To get an open look at the basket by overloading the zone on the baseline and playing a numbers game with the interior of the defense.

When to Use

When facing a standard 2-3 half-court zone defense, with normal shifts and movements, but not a matchup zone. However, it can be run only a possession at a time to counter the shifts of a basic 2-3 zone.

Key Personnel

All perimeter players should be good three-point shooters and able to get from the wings to the opposite corners quickly. The posts should be great power players and finishers.

Execution

1. 1 comes to the center of the zone to freeze the defense and passes to the wing on the side of whichever defender picks her up, in this case 3. 1 cuts below the free-throw line and then out to the opposite wing as 2 replaces her at the top of the key (figure 1).

2. 3 reverses the ball back to 2, who passes to 1 as 3 runs hard on the baseline to the opposite corner and 4 screens the middle of the zone. 5 steps out into the gap just outside the lane, looking for the pass from 1 (figure 2).

Points of Emphasis

This offense will get you an easy basket only after you have had good ball movement for multiple possessions, but timing and acting are key. The wings must convincingly call for the ball and cut underneath the zone to get the bottom defender to cheat out and cover her. At the same time, 4 must step in *big* to the center of the paint and post up the center of the zone. If the defender bites, 5 is left unguarded near the basket for an easy bucket.

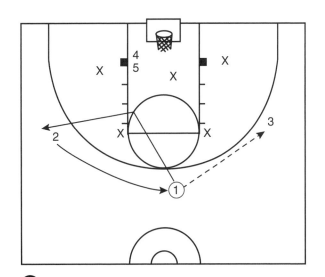

1

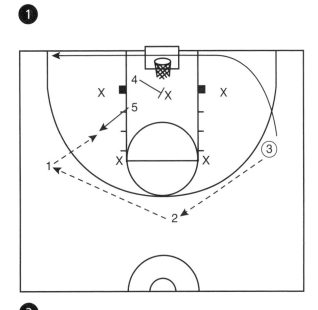

2

1-GUARD OFFENSE

Sylvia Hatchell

Objective

To take advantage of the gaps in the zone defense.

When to Use

Against two-guard front defenses such as the 2-3 and 1-2-1.

Key Personnel

The 4 should be the best passing forward and, along with 5, work well from both the elbow and the block. The 2 and 3 should have three-point range and be able to drive to the basket and make crisp skip passes.

Execution

1. 1 dribbles toward the gap between the two top defenders and passes either to 4 or to the open guard, in this case 2 (figure 1).

2. 2 looks to drive—for 5 posting up, 4 getting free in the ball-side elbow area, 3 finding open space on the help-side wing for the skip pass, or 1 relocating back to the top of the circle (figure 2).

3. If the ball reverses to 3, either through 1 or 4 or with the skip pass, 5 cuts diagonally to the opposite elbow and 4 cuts diagonally to the opposite block. 3 looks to shoot, drive, pass to 4 posting up, pass to 5 at the elbow, skip the ball back to 2, or pass to 1. Each time the ball reverses, 4 and 5 cut to the opposite block or elbow (figure 3).

Variations

- 2 sets a ball screen on the right side for 1, who sets up the screen by dribbling first with her left hand toward the defender and then switching to her right hand to brush off the screen. If the defender in the middle shifts to guard 2, 4 should be open (figure 4).

- When the ball reverses, 5 stays home on the low block. 2 slides down toward the corner. As 3 passes to 2, 5 posts up her player. 2 should be open for a shot, or 5 should be open for a feed (figure 5).

Points of Emphasis

The wings must not be on the same line as the wing defenders, instead splitting the gap between the top and bottom defenders. The wings should adjust their position on the floor to get open based on 1's dribble entry. 2 should look to shoot, but not on the first pass. This offense yields good shots if the offense is patient.

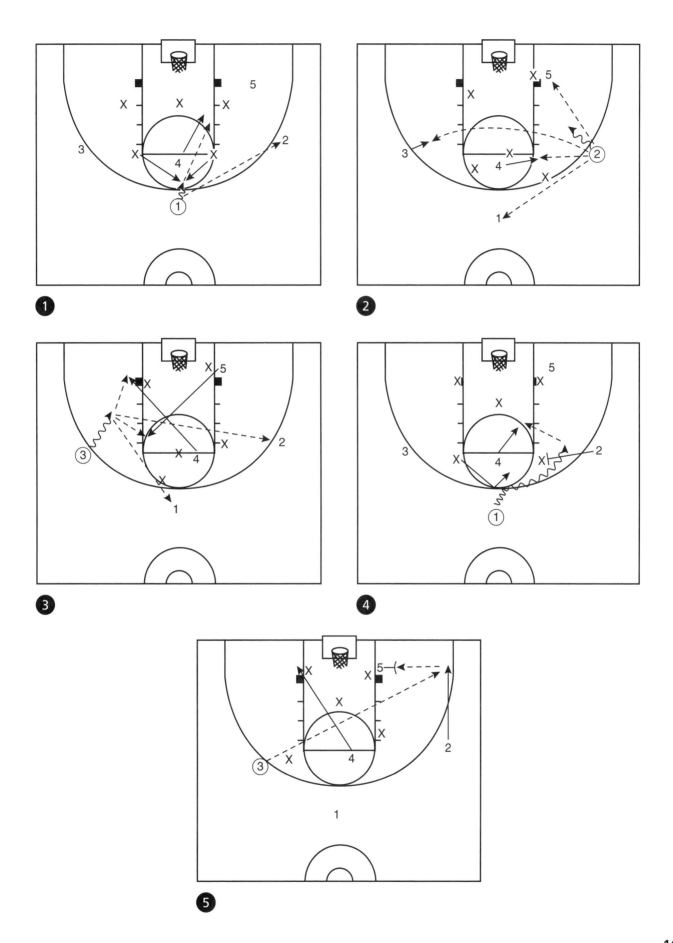

2-GUARD OFFENSE

Sylvia Hatchell

Objective

To take advantage of gaps in the zone defense.

When to Use

Against one-guard front defenses such as the 1-2-2 and 1-3-1.

Key Personnel

The 4 should be the best passing forward who also can shoot from the key and drive to the basket. The 2 should be able to hit the three-pointer. The 3 and 5 should be able to knock down the 15-footer and use screens effectively.

Execution

1. 1 dribbles toward the gap between the top defender and the elbow defender, in this case on the right side. She passes to 2, who will be open; to 3, who should be trying to sneak behind the defense; to 4 in the middle; or to 5 posting up (figure 1).

2. If 4 receives the ball, she shoots, passes to 3 or 5 if either is open, drives to the basket if she's given the lane, or passes to 2 (figure 2).

3. If 3 or 5 receives the ball, 4 sets a ball screen for the player with the ball or a back screen for the opposite short-corner player; cuts to the basket for a pass if she has an open lane; or calls for the ball back if she's wide open (figure 3).

Variation

4 screens the elbow defender. If 1 can't drive or shoot off the screen, 2 should be wide open (figure 4).

Points of Emphasis

The primary weakness of the 1-2-2 zone is in the middle, so 4 should be the first option regardless of who has the ball. The primary weakness of the 1-3-1 zone is along the baseline, so the short corners become the best option. One of the most effective passes is the diagonal pass between the wing and short corner because zone defenders are often so focused on the ball that they lose track of who is on the help side and who is behind them.

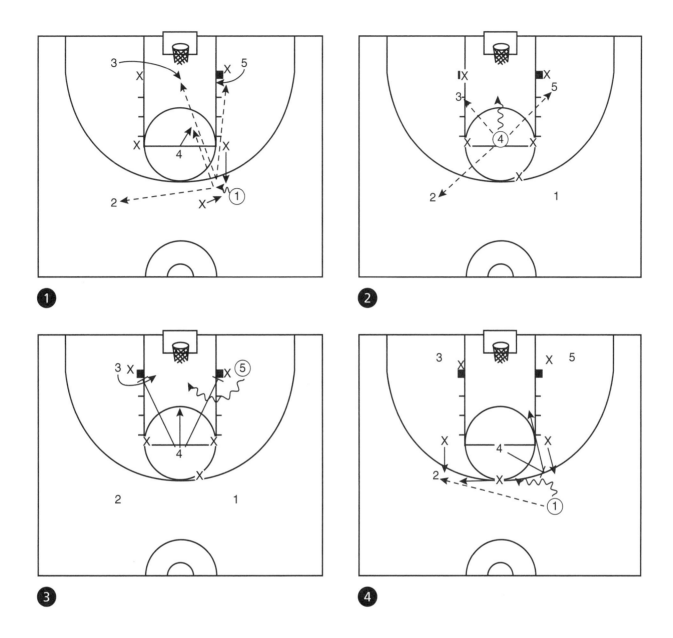

6

Perimeter Plays vs. Zone Defense

Zones can be divided into two general categories. An odd-front zone is one in which the number of players at the top of the zone is odd. The 1-3-1, 1-2-2, and 3-2 fall into that category. It makes sense, then, that an offense designed for an odd-front zone should begin with two perimeter players at the top, making the defense decide how to cover the personnel.

Conversely, an even-front zone is one in which the number of players at the top of the zone is even, such as a 2-3 or 2-1-2. In this case, the offense should begin with one perimeter player at the top, split between the two defenders.

Some plays work against any type of zone but that doesn't mean they should be run the same way against different alignments. The options will change based on which defense the opponent is in, but all these plays work best with excellent perimeter players who can penetrate the gaps in the zone and finish with a drive to the basket, if available, or else pass to the open player if two defenders are drawn. But even with average guards, these plays, if run well, can open up stronger post players. Perimeter players must be able to shoot the ball well off the dribble and from mid- and long range so defenders have reason to guard them outside. Players at the perimeter must screen and use screens well to create opportunities both for themselves and their teammates.

Passing is critical in these plays, which draw on the skip, reverse, and diagonal passes at various times. Acting also is important, with cuts, shot fakes, fake screens, and fake passes coming into play. And, of course, posts have their roles, too, be it via screening, providing outlets for easy buckets, popping out for unexpected long shots, flashing and rolling to the basket, making accurate passes, or working the boards.

The plays in this chapter are designed to create opportunities for the guards in several ways: by overloading areas of the zone so the defense can't cover every option, by drawing the next defender with a good shot fake to open up a driving lane or shot, by countering pre-rotation with a pass back, and by dribble attacking.

CORNER

Jennifer Rizzotti

Objective

To get a quick three-pointer for a shooter.

When to Use

- Against any kind of zone and to either side of the court, being aware of the direction the shooter likes to be going when she moves into a shot.
- When a quick three-pointer is needed late in the game.
- When a player has a hot hand from long range.

Key Personnel

The 2 player should be a shooter who can set her feet and knock down shots on the move. The 4 player must be able to shoot from 15 feet and make good passing decisions.

Execution

1. 1 dribbles to the wing as 2 shallow-cuts to the top of the key (figure 1).
2. 1 passes to 2, who then reverses the ball to 4. 4 hits 3 in the corner and then screens her defender while 2 cuts into the area 4 has vacated. 3 hits 2 for an open shot on the wing. If the defender jumps out to guard 2, 4 should be open inside the free-throw line for a jumper (figure 2).

Variations

- If the defender anticipates the screen and takes away the pass back to 2 on the wing, 3 needs to pass directly to 4, who should be open inside the three-point line.
- If the defense rotates to guard 4, 1 and 5, on opposite sides of the court, cut to an open spot in the zone. With the overload, someone on the weak side should be open.

Points of Emphasis

This play can probably be executed only once or twice a game before a good team adjusts to it, so it's best to save it for an opportune time, such as out of a timeout or at the end of a half or game. The surprise of the screen allows it to be successful, but once the defense is ready for it, it's not as effective.

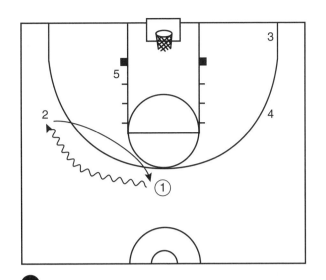

1

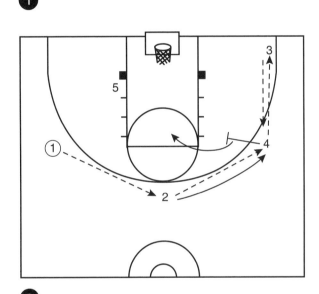

2

PITCH

Jennifer Rizzotti

Objective

To create an easy three-point shot.

When to Use

Against any zone on either side of the court, depending on which direction players prefer to attack off the ball screen, but not the corners.

Key Personnel

The 1 and 4 must make convincing fake passes to move the zone. The 2 must be able to shoot quickly on the move.

Execution

1. 1 passes to 4, who fakes a pass to 2 before passing back to 1. 1 fakes a pass to 3 before dribbling into the gap between her and 4 (figure 1).

2. As 1 drives, 4 steps down and sets a screen on the next player in the zone. 2 slides along the three-point line to the top of the key, where she receives a pitch back from 1 and shoots. 3, 4, and 5 crash the boards (figure 2).

Point of Emphasis

The keys to the play are moving the zone with good ball fakes and establishing personnel in the right spots.

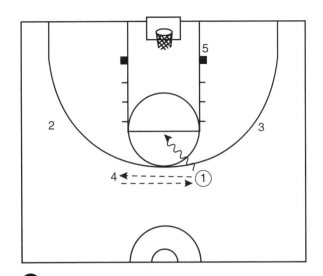

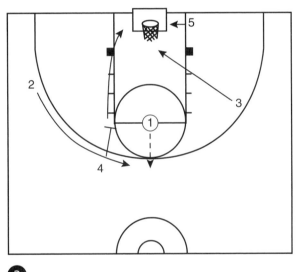

SCREEN

Jennifer Rizzotti

Objective

To create an easy scoring opportunity for the guards or a mid-post shot for the posts.

When to Use

Against a 2-3 or 3-2 zone on either side of the court, from whichever direction players prefer to attack off the ball screen.

Key Personnel

The 1 should be a good shooter, the 2 should attack well, and the 5 should be able to knock down a 12-foot jumper. The 3 should have a good shot fake to draw in the defense.

Execution

1. 1 passes to 2 and then cuts through to the opposite corner. 5 steps out to set a ball screen for 2 while 4 posts up on the weak-side block. 2 comes off the screen and attacks the middle of the floor while 3 slowly moves to the top of the key to receive the pass (figure 1).

2. 2 passes to 3 as 5 quickly rolls to the midpost. 4 moves to the short corner to prevent the defense from guarding two players in the zone. 3 looks at the basket to draw out a defender and then hits 1 in the corner or 5 in the key for a shot (figure 2).

Points of Emphasis

The 2 needs to come off a good screen aggressively and attack the middle of the zone, either creating a shot for herself or drawing the opposite guard defender. This forces the bottom defender to cheat up to guard the wing, allowing 1 to have an open look with crisp passing. The 5 must get to the midpost right after screening so the defense can't take her away when 3 has the ball.

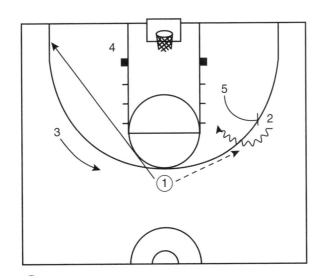

STACK

Jennifer Rizzotti

Objective

To create an easy scoring opportunity under the basket or an open shot in the corner.

When to Use

Against a 2-3 or 3-2 zone at any point of a game and to either side of the floor depending on which corner the shooter prefers and on which block the post is better at finishing.

Key Personnel

The 2 should be a great shooter the defense will worry about as she cuts through the bottom of the zone. The 4 needs to be a good passing post player who can make the right decision from the high post. The 5 should be a good finisher around the basket.

Execution

1. 1 passes to 2 on the wing and shifts toward her to receive the ball back. 2 returns the ball and then cuts to the opposite corner (figure 1).

2. 1 takes one or two dribbles back toward the top of the key as 3 cuts to the block and 4 cuts to just below the free-throw line. 1 passes to 4. 3 cross-screens for 5, who cuts to the opposite block. If the back of the zone takes away 5, 4 hits 2 in the corner. If the defender jumps out to guard 2, 5 or 3 should be wide open. If no one steps up to guard her, 4 shoots (figure 2).

Points of Emphasis

The 3 must understand who to screen in the zone. In a 2-3 set, it should be one of the bottom wing players. In a 3-2 zone, it should be whoever is matched up with 5. Also key is the location of 4's cut. If she cuts too high and the top players of the zone pick her up, the low defenders will be able to pick up the remaining players. Ideally, 4 pulls someone up from the bottom of the zone. If 3 screens well, it should leave only one player to guard both 3 and 5. 1 also needs to keep the top of the zone guarding her so they can't sag and take away the pass to 4.

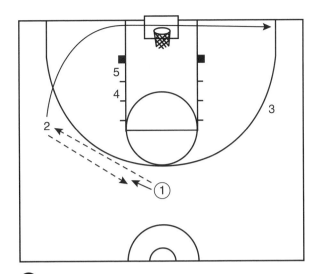

1

2

SHIFT

Jeff Walz

Objective

To shift the zone and get an open look on the opposite side of the court for a shooter.

When to Use

When defenders in a zone are ball watching a little too much.

Key Personnel

Against a 2-3 zone, you have two guards on the wings. The 1 must be able to throw a solid skip pass with strength and accuracy. The 3 must be able to set a solid zone screen. The 2 must have good timing in replacing 1 and have the ability to catch and shoot or to attack if the zone recovers. The posts must set good screens and roll and flash.

Execution

1. 1 passes to 3 and then switches places with 2 on the opposite wing. 4 pops out to the shallow corner ball side (figure 1).
2. 3 passes to 2, who passes to 1 (figure 2).
3. 3 and 4 screen the zone for 2, who receives a skip pass from 1 and looks for the shot (figure 3).

Variations

- After you have run the play once or twice, the defense might cheat, so fake the skip to draw the bottom zone defender out and pass to 4 slipping to the basket.
- If the top guard starts trying to cover the skip pass, 3 can flash to the middle of the zone for a short jumper.
- If the zone recovers, 1 might want to dribble pull-up, because the bottom of the zone might get screened but not the top.

Points of Emphasis

Screening the correct defender is important for 2 to receive the skip pass and have an open shot. The pass must be strong and accurate. A lobbed or telegraphed pass will break the play or cause a turnover. Player movement at the top of the key might cause some confusion, and the skip pass works great as long as it's a good one.

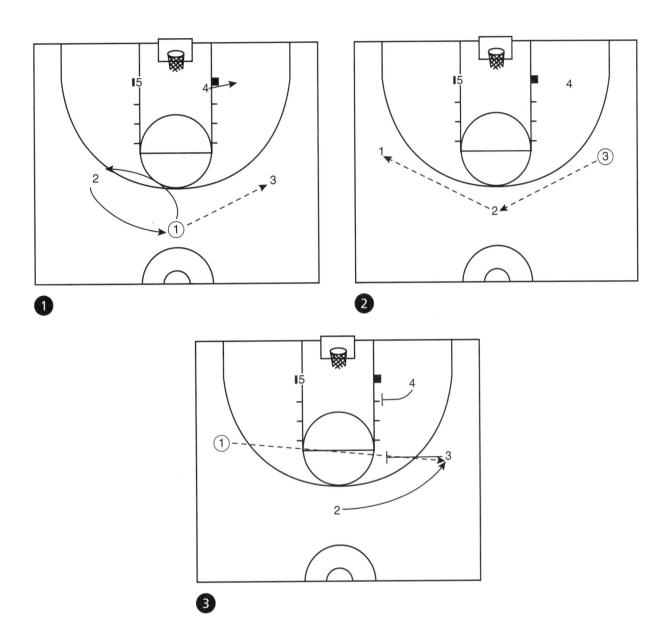

BASELINE

Sylvia Hatchell

Objective

To capitalize on great shooters at the wings.

When to Use

- Against all zones.
- To flatten a zone into a 2-3.

Key Personnel

You need excellent shooting guards at the wings.

Execution

1. 1 dribbles between the two players at the top of the zone. 2 and 3 move up the sideline slightly to be open for a pass, and 4 and 5 post up. 1 passes to whoever is open or dribbles back out to try again (figure 1).

2. If 2 or 3 receives the ball (in this case 2), she must read the defense. If 5's defender stays low, the wing has an open shot. If the defender comes out on 2, 5 should be open for a post feed. The wing also can skip the ball to the opposite wing, or if the defender at the top of the zone drops to cover the wing, 1 should cut into the open space for the pass (figure 2).

Points of Emphasis

Having players in the corners forces any zone to flatten out into a 2-3 formation. The ball on the wing creates a dilemma for 5's defender. If the defender goes out to guard 2, 5 should be open for a post feed. If she stays on 5, 2 has the open shot.

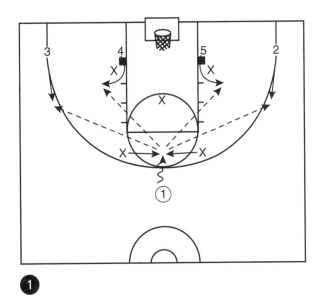

1

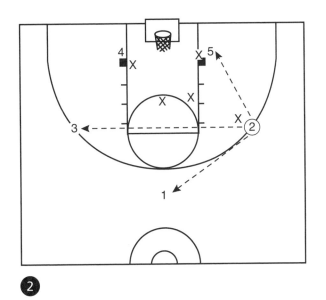

2

OVERLOAD

Sylvia Hatchell

Objective

To have more offensive players in an area than there are defenders, presenting a 3-on-2 or 2-on-1 situation.

When to Use

Against all zones.

Key Personnel

The 1 needs good range from the corner. The 4 and 5 should work well from both the elbow and the block. The 2 and 3 should have three-point range and be able to drive to the basket and make crisp skip passes.

Execution

1. 1 passes to 2 and then cuts to the ball-side corner through the center of the lane while 3 moves to the top of the circle (figure 1).

2. 2 can shoot, drive, or pass to 1 in the corner, 5 posting up, 4 in the high post, or to 3 at the top of the key (figure 2).

3. If 1 receives the ball and doesn't shoot, she can pass to 5 posting up, to 4 who's posting up or cutting to the basket, skip it to 3, or pass back to 2, who has the same options as before (figure 3).

4. If the ball reverses, from 1 to either 2 or 3, 1 cuts to the opposite corner, 4 and 5 cut diagonally to the opposite elbow and block, respectively, and 2 spots on the perimeter midway between the wing and the top of the circle, and the play continues (figure 4).

Point of Emphasis

The 1 will usually be wide open in the corner.

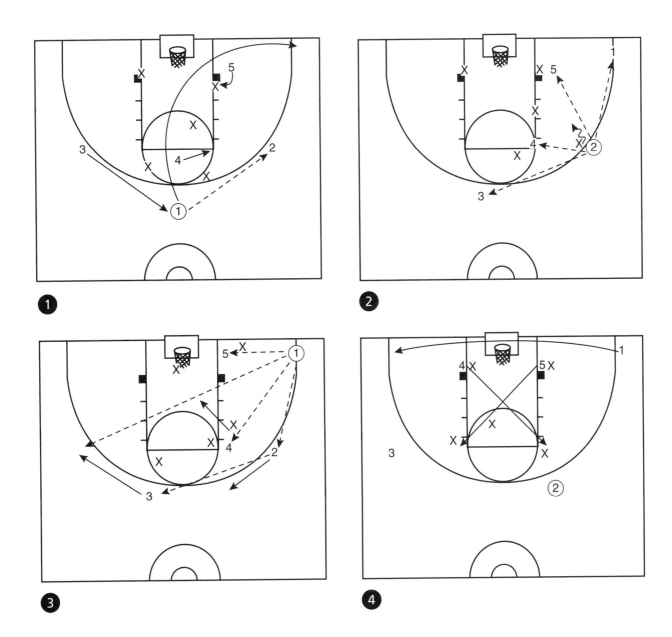

CUTTERS

June Daugherty

Objectives

- To create a two-on-one situation.
- To get a quick three-point shot.

When to Use

Against an even-front zone, such as a 2-3 or 2-1-2.

Key Personnel

Your 4 must be a post player who can step out and hit a three.

Execution

1. As 1 dribbles into position outside the three-point line, 4 and 5 move up their lanes to the top of the key. 1 passes to the weaker post shooter, in this case 5, as 2 and 3 cut in and then out to their respective wings (figure 1).

2. 1 cuts in either direction (in this case left) and 3 clears to the opposite baseline. 5 hits 4, who has stepped out beyond the three-point line and then cuts low to hold the mid-defender. 2 cuts on the wing to keep the defender distracted (figure 2).

3. 4 shoots or fakes a shot, hits 2, and then cuts through the lane to the weak-side block. 2 shoots or fakes a shot and hits 3. After each pass, the passer cuts through the lane to the baseline, shifting the perimeter players over one spot (figure 3).

Points of Emphasis

Each perimeter player must draw the next defender with a good shot fake and be a viable threat from beyond the arc. Otherwise, the defenders can cheat off and pre-rotate. Passes should arrive on the shooting shoulder of the receiver so she can catch and shoot in rhythm. If the defense is rotating to the pass and playing show-release—that is, showing to the ball without ever getting into a defined defensive position relative to the offensive player, which allows them to release to the pass and arrive at the receiver in time to prevent an open shot—pass back in the direction the last pass came from.

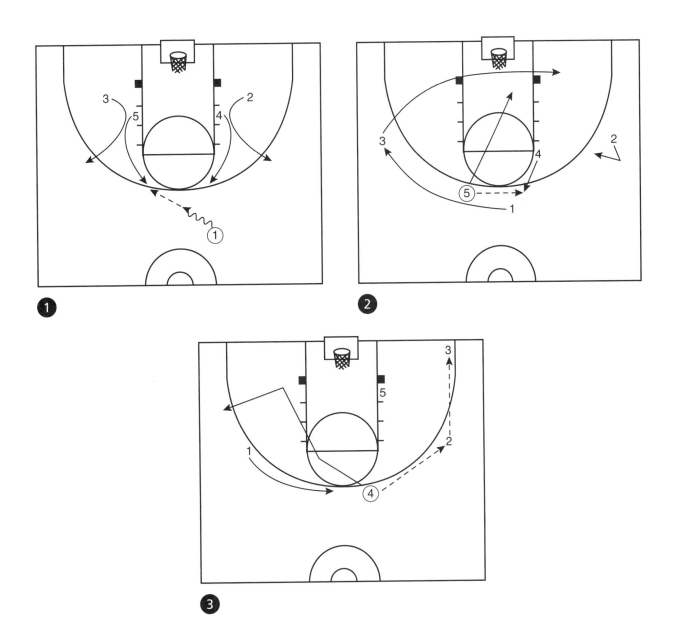

DOWN

June Daugherty

Objective

To overload areas in the zone so the defense can't cover all options.

When to Use

Against any zone set.

Key Personnel

For this play to be effective inside, you need a playmaker in the short corner, three-point spot-up shooters, and players who can read a spread floor and make good decisions. The 4 is your best post playmaker. The 1 is your most intelligent player, though not necessarily your point guard because players can switch places upon dribble entry or the first pass.

Execution

1. 1 dribbles to the right wing as 2 clears via the baseline to the opposite sideline halfway between the corner and the wing. The ball reverses from 4 to 3 to 2. 5 drops down the lane before cutting to the short baseline (figure 1).

2. 2 fakes a shot to draw out the low defender and then looks for 5 or 4 cutting through the midpost gap. 3 clears to the weak-side block (figure 2).

3. If nothing is there, 2 dribbles up to the wing and looks again to 5 before reversing the ball to 1 at the top of the key. 4 fills the gap on the other side of the lane as 3 moves up to the wing (figure 3).

4. 4 and 5 cut up their sides of the lane to the gap, and 3 drops into the gap between the wing and the corner. With 2, 3, 4, and 5 in zone gaps and only three defenders to cover them, 1 hits the open player (figure 4).

5. If 1 passes to 4 or 5, the other post dives to the basket looking for a quick pass. If 1 passes to 2 or 3, 4 and 5 fill the short corner and midpost gap, and 2 shifts toward the top of the key as an outlet (figure 5).

Variations

- Against a 2-3 zone, 1 can draw the top guard defender to the wing before reversing the ball. Then, as the defense shifts, she makes sure she's looking back the same way as the ball came from after the initial ball reversal to the top to stop the defense from rotating too quickly.

- Against a 1-2-2 or 1-3-1 zone, 4 is in the gap between the weak-side top defenders and the ball is pounded into her or into 5.

Points of Emphasis

Fakes, the use of the short corner, and an initial quick ball reversal are critical to this play's success. The 2 must draw the low defender with a good shot fake, which should be used convincingly after every pass thereafter. Pass fakes away from the intended target also keep the defense off balance. The 5 needs to be aggressive in shooting the ball off a drop-step jumper or in driving the baseline to the basket, recognizing that 4 should be open if the defense collapses on her. When 1 shot-fakes at the top of the key, she reads the defense and passes to the side of whichever guard bites. Finally, players on the weak side crash the boards to overload the rebounding position.

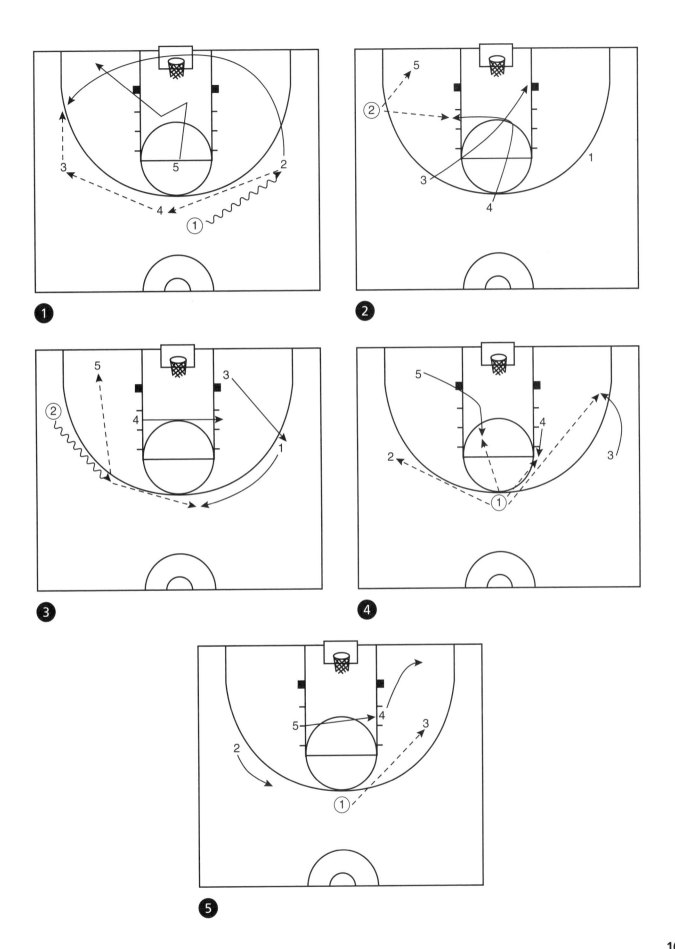

GAPS

June Daugherty

Objective

To cause a zone to rotate to the ball and then attack the gaps, leaving the next player with the ball open to shoot or to attack a wider gap.

When to Use

- Against a 2-3 or 1-2-2 zone.
- For a quick three-point shot in a short-second situation.

Key Personnel

The more players on the floor who can catch and shoot from three-point range, the less likely the zone can cheat off a particular player and pre-rotate the zone. This play also works with slashers, who use slashing movements to attack gaps and get inside the zone.

Execution

1. 1 dribbles to the wing, clearing 2 to the opposite corner. 5 steps out, staying within her range, and 4 (the trailing post) sets a ball screen for 1. 1 drives off the screen and reads the defense. If the defender follows under the screen, 1 kicks the ball back to 4. If the opposite guard shifts to help, 1 passes to 3 (figure 1).

2. If 3 gets the ball, she makes the low defender commit to her with a shot, shot fake, or drive. If the defender bites, 3 dumps to 2. If the defender doesn't bite, 3 shoots. If the defense rotates successfully to guard 2 and 3, 3 hits 1 cutting through the midpost gap (figure 2).

3. If still nothing, 3 attacks the up-gap with a drive or drag dribble as 2 fills her spot and 1 drops to the corner. 3 then passes back to 2, if the defender follows her, or to 4 if the next defender shifts to help. The play continues as such (figure 3).

Variations

- If used against an odd-front zone, the emphasis changes to getting the ball to the guard cutting into the middle gap after the perimeter pass.
- Against a 1-2-2, after 1 clears to the corner, 3 cuts to the midpost gap for the pass as 4 moves to the top of the key as an outlet (figure 4).

Points of Emphasis

The player on the wing can be 1, 2, or 3. The play can be run so the best penetrator and passer has the ball first, and the best shooter receives the first pass. The gap penetrators must be able to attack the zone off the dribble and then read the defense to make the appropriate next pass. They must also be able to make an accurate pass in either direction off a drag dribble by creating space with their footwork. The wing must draw the next defender up to her with a great shot-fake or jab step to prevent the defense from pre-rotating. This should leave the baseline open. Players remain spaced at 12 to 15 feet (3.6-4.5 m) to prevent a defender from guarding two players. Passes arrive on the shoulder side of the receiver so shooters can release in rhythm and on balance. Weak-side rebounders must establish position as soon as they recognize open shooters receiving the ball.

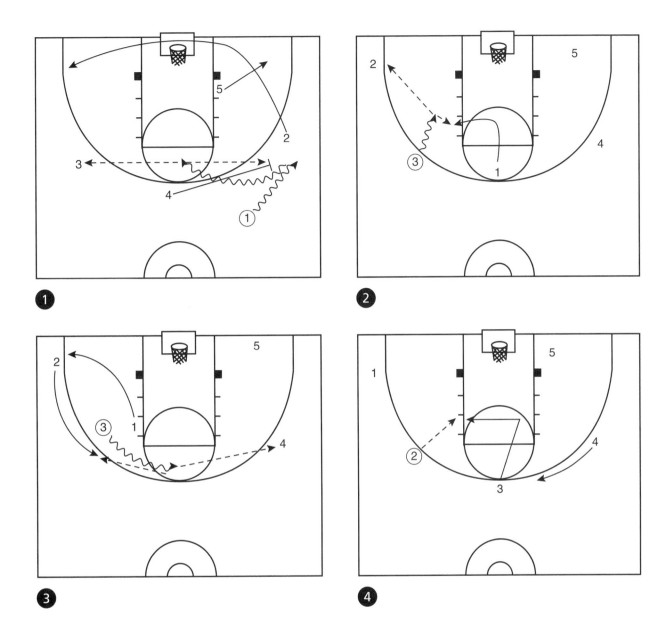

BOX THREE

June Daugherty

Objective

To attack a 1-2-2 zone by getting the ball in the middle of the paint.

When to Use

When a team's basic attack needs a fresh look.

Key Personnel

The 3 is your player most effective in traffic. The 2 is a good shooter, and 5 is a big target.

Execution

1. 1 dribbles to the arc in the gap in the zone. 2 holds a defender and then cuts to the baseline. 1 passes to 4. 2 continues to the halfway point between the weak-side corner and the wing as 3 cuts around 5 to the midpost gap and 5 drops to the baseline. 4's first look is to 3, and then to 2 (figure 1).

2. If 3 gets the ball, she looks to score or kicks it out to an open player. 5 dives to the hoop for the rebound as 1 and 4 drop inside the three-point line (figure 2).

3. If 2 gets the ball, 3 finds the open gap and 5 holds the low defender. 3 and 5 rebound weak side if 2 shoots.

Points of Emphasis

The 1 and 4 need to be in the gaps in the three-defender top. The 2 must time her arrival on the weak side to be ready to shoot when 4 makes the pass but should not arrive too early and give the defense time to rotate. The 4 fakes a pass to 2 before hitting 3, and 3 squares up to make a play depending on what the defense gives her.

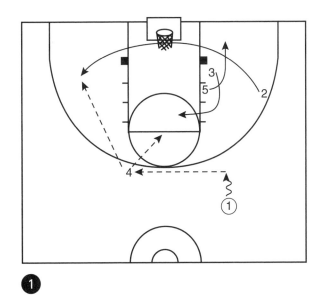

1

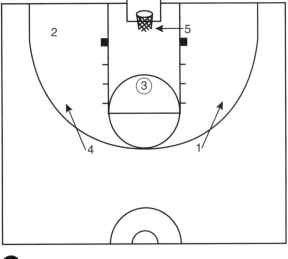

2

UP SCREEN

June Daugherty

Objectives

- To create a quick scoring opportunity.
- To get the post an inside look.

When to Use

As a change-up to an expected offensive set.

Key Personnel

The 2 is a very good shooter on the wing. The 1 can shoot well off the dribble.

Execution

1. 5 comes outside the three-point line to set a pick for 1, who drives to the wing looking to score or draw up the low defender. 5 drops to the ball-side block, sealing her defender and looking for a quick pass. 2 cuts out and then to the corner, and 3 pops out to the wing. 4 shifts over, ready for a pass from 1 if the defender beats the pick (see the figure).

2. If 1 doesn't have a shot, she reads the defense and makes a pass to 2 or 4 depending on which defender is guarding her.

Points of Emphasis

The 1 must be aggressively looking to score coming off the pick. That's the first option, and the purpose of the play. If she doesn't shoot, she must at least drive hard enough to draw up the low defender before passing to 2 on the baseline.

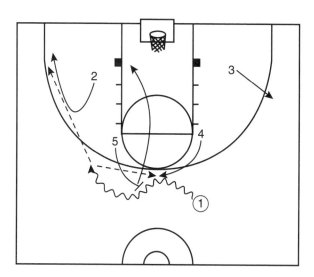

WAVE

Jennifer Rizzotti

Objective

To create a scoring opportunity in the high-post area or a high-low pass for a layup.

When to Use

Against any zone as long as players are cutting to open areas, which might vary based on the defense. The play can be run to either side of the court.

Key Personnel

The 3 is a midrange, triple-threat player with some size. The 2 is a good decision maker and passer. The 4 and 5 are active players good at finishing around the basket.

Execution

1 dribbles to the opposite wing of the player cutting, in this case toward 2, who at the same time shallow-cuts to the top of the key. When 1 arrives to the wing, 3 cuts to an open area at the mid- or high post. 4 and 5 are in their respective short corners, ready for a pass. 1 ball fakes to 2 or 4 before passing to 3, who can shoot, drive, or feed a post (see the figure).

Variations

- Against a 2-3 zone, 5 might match up with the guard, which could create a driving opportunity.
- In a 3-2 zone, one of the back post defenders could come up to guard the high post, which leaves 4 or 5 open for a high-low pass.

Points of Emphasis

The 3 must do a great job making her initial cut toward the ball. It can't be to a specific spot but rather to whatever area is open. The 3 must be a good decision maker who can determine which option is the best available on the catch. The 1's ball fake should shift the defense and further open up the high-post area for 3.

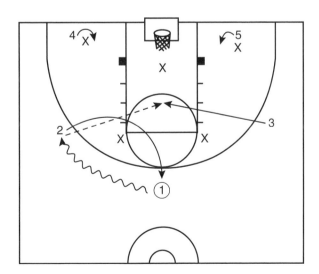

7

Out-of-Bounds Plays

Basketball is generally a continuous-action sport, with play transitioning from offense to defense and defense to offense even after a team scores unless an opponent presses. The exceptions are when a period ends, when an official calls a foul, when the ball goes out of bounds, when a time-out is called, and when an unusual stoppage of play is required. At these times teams can set up a play for their offense with the luxury of an idle defense.

As any basketball coach knows, out-of-bounds plays can significantly affect the outcome of a game. Not counting the inbounds passes that follow a score by the opponent, a team might inbound the ball one to two dozen times a game. Assuming each possession is worth only two points, a team could easily score 20 to 40 points a game off the sets—certainly enough to win or lose the contest.

A team can take the ball out-of-bounds virtually anywhere on the court along a baseline or sideline. The sets in this chapter address each possible scenario, but in every case the inbounds player must be able to read the defense, determine its set, and call a corresponding play.

The plays in this chapter cover every conceivable inbounds objective: scoring or getting the ball in safely, featuring every player on the court in at least one set or option, with just a few ticks or many left on the game clock and shot clock, both against man-to-man and zone defenses, when the offense has a significant size mismatch at a particular position, when a defending post player is in foul trouble, and for layups and three-pointers and everything in between.

The fundamentals of basketball remain important on out-of-bounds plays—great decision-making, precise passing, posting up, screening, finishing in traffic, outside shooting—although different plays require these skills to varying degrees.

An important consideration when compiling your repertoire of out-of-bounds plays is, to the extent possible, they have similar initial alignments prior to live action. Obviously, if each inbounds play calls for a different setup, the opponent will be tipped off on which play you're planning to run.

Another strategy when designing out-of-bounds plays, especially those underneath the offensive basket, is to create as much nonpositional screening as possible, meaning a post screens a guard's defender or vice versa. This makes it more difficult for the opponent to switch defenders or to guard effectively in the resulting matchup.

BIG GUN

Audra Smith

Objective

To isolate a post player for a quick layup under the basket.

When to Use

- When only a few seconds remain on the shot clock.
- Against a man-to-man defense.

Key Personnel

Your 4 is your best passer. Your 5 is your most aggressive post player, good at pinning and sealing the defense. Your guards must be good shooters so the defense must guard them tight on the perimeter.

Execution

5 turns and sets a strong screen for 3, who pops out to the three-point line, while 2 pops to the opposite corner and 1 pops to the top of the key. 5 immediately seals her defender, and 4 passes directly to 5 for the layup (see the figure).

Points of Emphasis

The 5 must set a good screen for 3, who must wait for the screen and then come off it as if she's about to get the ball. The 1 and 2 also sprint to their positions with intention. The play breaks down if 3 moves before the screen is set and 5 does not seal the defender.

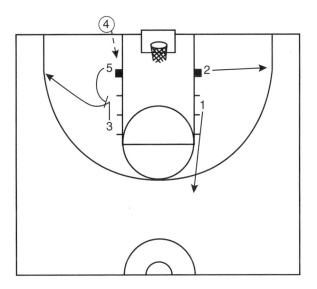

BLAST

Audra Smith

Objective

To get 2 a quick shot, 3 a short corner jumper, or 4 a post-up opportunity.

When to Use

At any time in the game against a man-to-man defense.

Key Personnel

Your 2 is your best shooter. Your 3 is a strong guard who can come off screens hard. Your 4 is a great post-up player and your 5 a high-post threat; both should be good at setting screens.

Execution

1. 2 comes off a double screen by 4 and 5 as 1 rotates over to the opposite wing. 3 hits 2 for a quick shot (figure 1).

2. If 2 is not open, she dribbles toward the top of the arc and reverses the ball to 1. 4 and 5 move down to the block to set a double screen for 3, who curls to the corner. 1 looks to hit 3 for a layup or on the baseline for a jumper (figure 2).

3. If 3 doesn't have a scoring opportunity, 4 curls off 5 to the opposite block and posts up, looking to score, and 5 moves to the high post looking for a pass (figure 3).

Points of Emphasis

The play's success is determined by the screening, the scoring ability of the players, and timing. The 2 must go shoulder to shoulder with her teammates to get open. The 4 and 5 must move to the block quickly to set up the double screen for 3, who must be patient and not come off the screen too soon. She might have a mismatch if the defender on 4 or 5 picks her up off the screen. If so, 4 might also benefit from a mismatch. The 1 must have the ball as 3 is curling off 4 and 5. The 5 must be patient to allow 4 to curl before going to the high post.

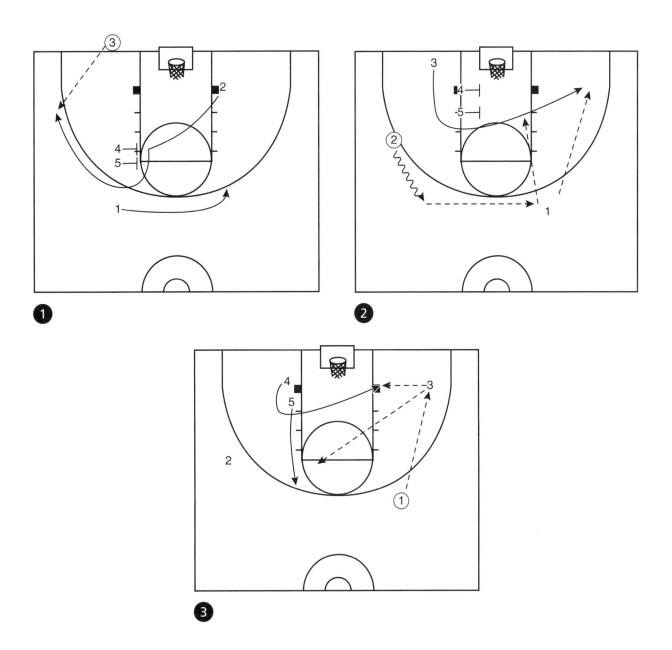

CHOMP

Audra Smith

Objective

To obtain a quick shot for 1, a three-pointer for 2, or an eventual look for 3.

When to Use

Against a man-to-man defense.

Key Personnel

The three guards must be proficient at shooting and in reading and setting up screens.

Execution

1. 1 sets a screen for 2, popping to the corner before rolling off a double screen by 4 and 5. 3 inbounds the ball to 1, who looks for an immediate jumper (figure 1).

2. If 1 is not open, 4 and 5 set a stagger screen for 2, who receives the ball from 1 above the arc for a three-point shot (figure 2).

3. If 2 isn't open, 4 and 5 double-screen on the block for 3, who receives the ball in the short corner from 2 (figure 3).

4. If no shot opportunity arises, 4 goes to the high post and 5 stays on the low block for a high-low option (figure 4).

Points of Emphasis

Ideally, this play is designed for the 1 to get a quick bucket, considering the defense must fight through a double screen by two post players, but its most important aspects are timing and screening. Posts must set solid screens, but not too soon, and guards must brush tight off the screen to lose their defender.

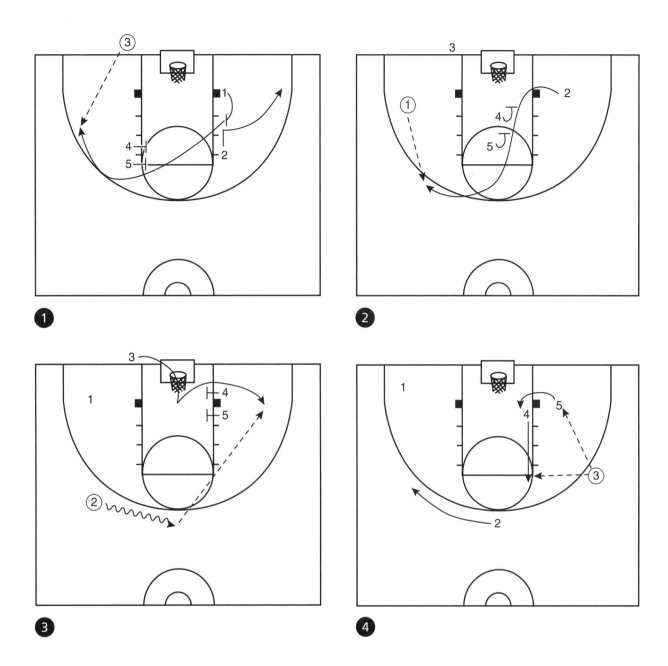

DOUBLE UP

Audra Smith

Objectives

- To get a layup for 5 or an immediate jumper for 3.
- To provide multiple scoring options.

When to Use

- Against a man-to-man defense at any point during a game.
- With a dominant post player and good perimeter scorers.
- Against opponents that have trouble defending screens.

Key Personnel

This play requires three good scorers who set up and read screens effectively. Your 5 must be able to set good screens.

Execution

1. 3 sets a strong back screen for 5, who comes off looking for the layup. 3 then comes off a screen from 4, looking for a jumper on the wing (figure 1).
2. If neither opportunity exists, 3 reverses the ball to 4, who swings the ball to 1 coming up from the corner (figure 2).
3. 2 has the option of heading to the top of the key off a stagger screen by 3 and 4 or to the opposite corner off 5's single screen (figure 3).

Point of Emphasis

All three aspects of screening are critical to the success of this play: the technique of setting the screen, the timing of the screen, and using the screen.

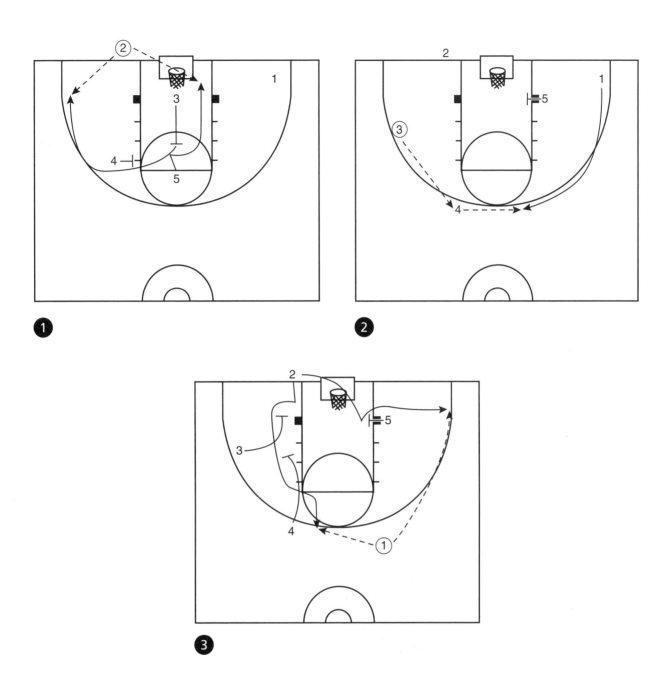

BACK

Deb Patterson

Objective

To use back screens as potential scoring opportunities.

When to Use

Against teams in a man-to-man defense that do not like to switch screens.

Key Personnel

Your 4 should have good pick-and-pop scoring skills.

Execution

1. On the ball slap, 4 turns to set a diagonal back screen for 3, who cuts hard across the lane to the ball-side block. 1 looks to 3 for a layup. As 3 cuts, 5 pops hard to the ball-side wing. If 3 isn't open, 1 passes to 5 on the wing and fills the ball-side corner. As 5 catches, 4 turns to bump-screen 2, who is cutting hard to the top of the key (figure 1).

2. 5 passes to 2. 4 steps up to set a ball screen for 2 as 3 steps off the block and diagonal back-screens for 5, who cuts to the basket. 2 dribbles off the screen to the wing and passes to 5 or 4 popping off the screen (figure 2).

Points of Emphasis

A bump screen is simply a very quick down screen. The 2 must be a three-point threat. She also needs to come off the ball screen hard, looking to turn the corner. The 4 must be able to shoot the three.

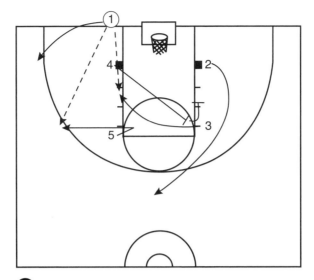

1

2

FLAT

Deb Patterson

Objective

To center the ball and create a threat on both sides of the court.

When to Use

- Against a man-to-man defense when you want to pressure the defense by driving to the rim.
- When looking for a three-point opportunity.

Key Personnel

This play is oriented to the dribble game and to perimeter players. 4 or 5 must be able to take two dribbles without bobbling the ball.

Execution

1. On the ball slap, 3, 4, and 5 cut high to 15 feet (4.5 m) from a post-up seal position, showing a high outside target hand. 1 passes to 5 and then steps into the ball-side block. 4 sets a down screen for 1, who curls and accepts a dribble-weave handoff from 5 (figure 1).

2. As the dribble-weave begins, 3 dives back down to the weak-side block and then runs off a 4-5 stagger screen as 1 turns the corner and drives to the rim. If 1 is pushed back on penetration, she passes either to 3 or, if 2's defender helped on 1's drive, to 2 (figure 2).

Points of Emphasis

The dribble-weave between 5 and 1 must be well-executed. 1 looks to turn the corner if she can and attack the basket. 2 must be ready for the three-point shot.

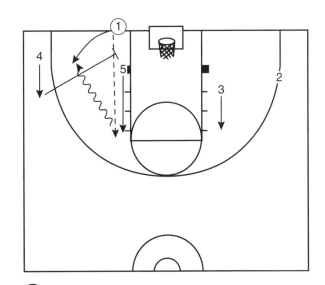

1

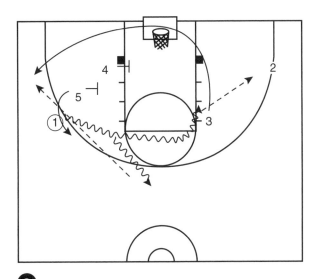

2

BIG

Deb Patterson

Objectives

- To create a high-percentage shot at the rim.
- To stretch the defense and maximize the opportunity for a post mismatch or isolation.

When to Use

- Against a man-to-man defense when the offense has a size or skill advantage at the 5 spot.
- When the opponent's post defender is in foul trouble.

Key Personnel

Your 4 should be a threat from three-point range. Your 5 should be a strong back-to-the-basket scorer.

Execution

1. On the ball slap, 3 sets a screen on 4's defender while 4 cuts hard to the ball-side baseline. At the same time, 5 turns to the inside to screen 2's defender while 2 makes a diagonal cut to the weak-side baseline at the three-point line, calling for the ball the entire time. 5's screen should move her to the middle of the lane at the free-throw line. 1 passes to 4 unless 3, who has stepped in and then popped hard to the ball-side wing, is open (figure 1).

2. 4 passes to 3. 1 then steps under the basket and waits for 5 to set a screen in the middle of lane so 1 can bust to the top of the key. 5 seals her defender. 3 passes to 1 as 2 cuts hard to the wing. 1 hits 5 in a post-up isolation in the lane or immediately passes it to 2, who hits 5 on a post seal (figure 2).

Points of Emphasis

The more closely 2, 3, and 4 must be guarded as three-point shooters, the greater the probability of creating a strong post isolation. Against a team that switches defensively in inbounds plays, 5 should have a mismatch against a guard. The 5 must demand the ball and be a big target once 1 or 2 receives the pass.

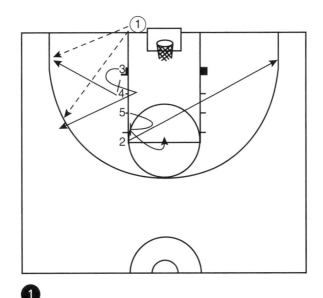

1

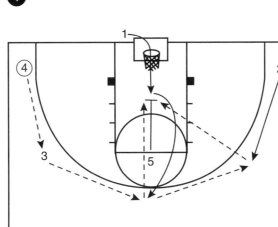

2

READ

Deb Patterson

Objectives

- To provide at least three good scoring opportunities.
- To exploit an early switch on defenses that show and chase hard on down screens.

When to Use

- Against man-to-man teams that have a mismatch in size at the 3.
- With 15 or more seconds on the shot clock.

Key Personnel

Your 3 should be big and an equal threat to score on the block or from behind the arc. Your 4 should be a three-point threat who forces defenses to chase or show.

Execution

1. On the ball slap, 4 sets a cross-screen for 1, who cuts hard to the ball-side corner. 2 passes to 1, then runs to the ball-side wing. Meanwhile, 3 down-screens at about 13 feet (3.9 m) for 4. As 4 cuts up the lane to the top of the key as a three-point threat, 1 passes to 2. 3 and 5 then read the defense (figure 1).

2. Option A: If the defense shows on 4, 3 slips to the block for the pass from 2 (figure 2).

3. Option B: 5 screens for 3, who pops out to the weak-side wing. 2 passes to 3 or 4. 4 can shoot from the top of the key. 3 can shoot or drive to the rim, with 4 trailing. 5 and 2 set a weak-side stagger screen for 1, who fills the top of the key (figure 3).

Points of Emphasis

This is a "screen the screener" play, so screens must be solid. Ideally, 4 can shoot the three. The 5 sets a flare screen but needs to read the defense, looking for a slip to the basket. If the slip isn't there, 5 looks for the skip pass. The right side is overloaded so 3 can drive.

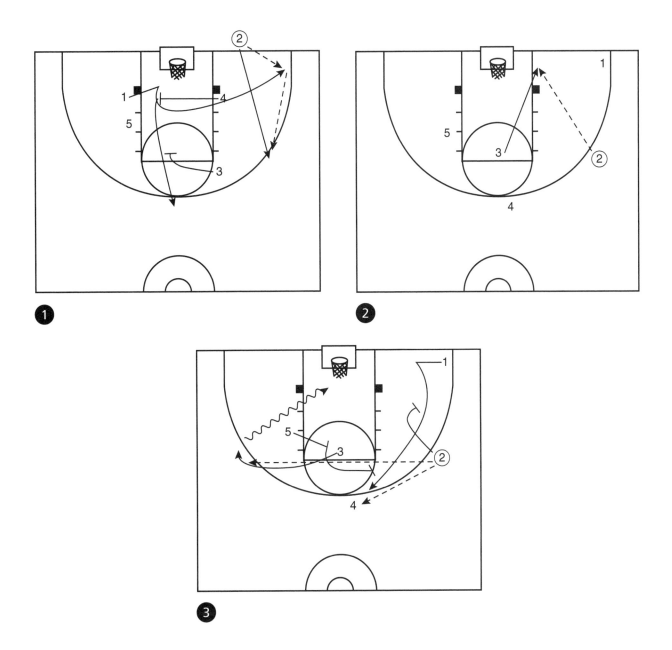

WIDE

Deb Patterson

Objective

To create both two- and three-point scoring opportunities.

When to Use

- Against a man-to-man team that likes to show strong with their ball-side defender on a double-down screen.

- When a lot of time is left on the shot clock.

- To create continuity and a variety of scoring opportunities throughout a possession.

Key Personnel

Post players should be effective at reading defenses and working in tandem with one another.

Execution

1. On the ball slap, 2 cuts to the ball-side block and then continues through the lane to the weak-side baseline at the three-point line. 4 and 5 turn to stagger screen 3's defender as 3 runs fast and tight to the ball-side wing. 1 passes to 3. Immediately after the catch, 1 steps under the basket and runs off a double screen at 14 feet (4.2 m) by 4 and 5. 3 and 5 read the ball-side post defender. If she shows as 1 cuts off the screen, 5 slips to the ball-side block and receives the pass from 3 (figure 1).

2. If 5 is not open, 3 passes to 1 at the three-point line or to 2 on the opposite wing. 1 shoots or reverses the ball to 2. If 2 catches on the reversal, 4 dives to the block and 5 cuts to the high post for a high-low game. 1 and 3 fill the weak-side baseline and wing (figure 2).

Point of Emphasis

The 4 and 5 players must set solid stagger screens and then a wall screen for 1.

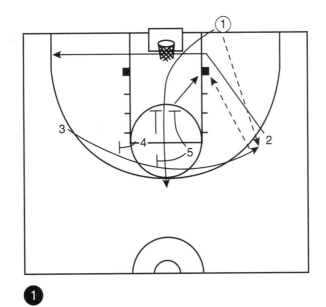

1

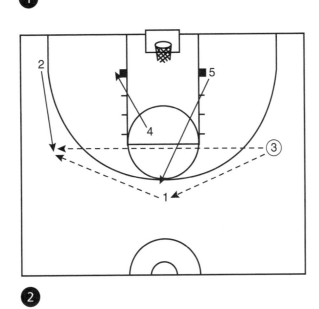

2

BASELINE DOWN

Beth Burns

Objectives

- To provide scoring options for a perimeter shooter and low-block scorers.
- To spread the defense, making it difficult to cover the initial alignment on the inbounds play.

When to Use

- Against a man-to-man defense, especially a switching defense.
- In short-second situations.

Key Personnel

Your 1 should be a precision passer who can hit the three from the corner. Your 2 must be a great catch-and-shoot player who can free herself off a stagger screen. Your 3 should be a good perimeter shooter who can spread the defense and reverse the ball. Your 4 should be the best screener and a good low-block finisher. Your 5 must be a good screener and your best low-block scorer with ability to finish in traffic with contact.

Execution

1. On the ball slap, 5 and 4 set a stagger screen for 2, who heads to the ball-side wing. 3 flashes to the top of the key as a safety valve (figure 1).
2. 5 and 4 continue across the lane until 5 cuts back to use 4's screen to curl to the basket or to post up her defender. 1 has three primary options—hitting 2, 4, or 5—before releasing to the weak-side corner (figure 2).
3. If 2 receives the ball, she passes to 3, who then hits 5 after she pins her defender (figure 3).

Points of Emphasis

The two post players must set good screens, and the 2 guard must cut tight off the screens so her defender is delayed. If the 2 guard can't get open, the play dies and the safety outlet is used.

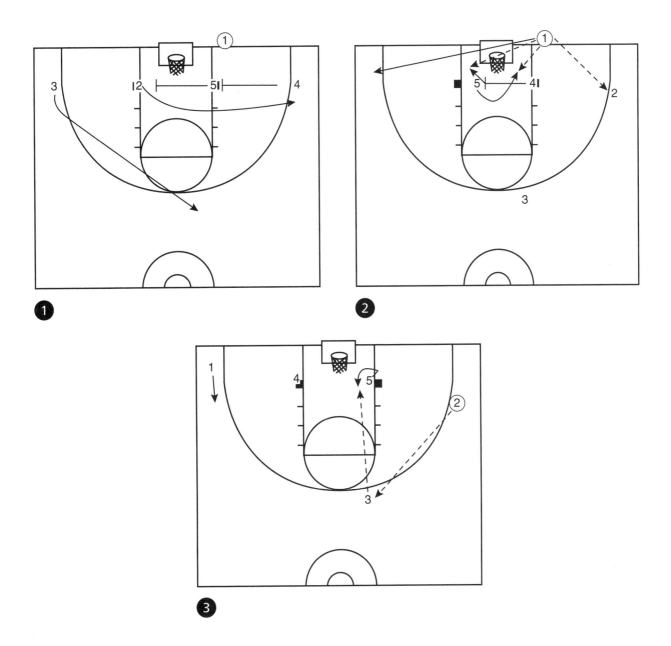

BASELINE MIDDLE

Beth Burns

Objectives

- To provide a scoring option for a perimeter shooter and low-post scorer.
- To spread the defense, making it difficult to cover the initial alignment on the inbounds play.

When to Use

- Against a man-to-man defense, especially a switching defense.
- In short-second situations.
- After using Baseline Down a few times.

Key Personnel

Your 1 should be a precision passer. Your 2 needs to be a good catch-and-shoot player on the perimeter. Your 3 should be a threat from behind the arc to stretch the defense. Your 4 must set good screens and be able to duck in and score on the low block. Your 5 is your best low-post scorer who can finish in traffic with contact.

Execution

1. On the ball slap, 2 cross-screens for 5. 1 feeds 5 for an easy bucket if she's open (figure 1).
2. If not, 4 cross-screens for 2, who receives the pass from 1 at the wing and looks to shoot. 3 flashes to the top of the key for a safety valve (figure 2).

Points of Emphasis

A good solid screen by 2 on 5 causes 2's defender to help on the screen. This allows 4 to set a quick, hard screen to get 2 open to the wing for a shot. Without a good screen from 2, the play won't be successful.

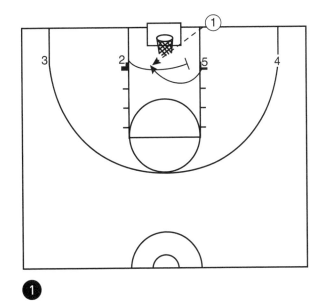

①

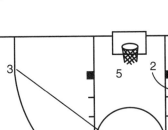

②

SQUARE 1

Beth Burns

Objectives

- To provide scoring options from several areas on the floor.
- To safely inbound the ball.

When to Use

Against a man-to-man defense.

Key Personnel

The 1 should be a precision passer and able to shoot the three. The 2 should be your best perimeter shooter and proficient at setting a back screen. The 3 should be a big guard, able to finish in traffic and a perimeter threat to stretch the defense. The 4 needs to be a great screener with ability to score off the duck-in. The 5 is your best low-post scorer, able to catch and finish in traffic, and a good screener.

Execution

1. On the ball slap, 2 up-screens for 3, who cuts to the weak-side block (figure 1).
2. 2 uses an elevator screen by 4 and 5 to get to the ball-side wing, where she receives the pass from 1. 2 looks to shoot or feed 5 slipping to the basket if 5's defender followed 2. 3 spaces to the weak-side wing (figure 2).
3. If 2 doesn't shoot, she passes to 1, who has flashed up the lane to the top of the key off 4's screen. 4 continues from the screen to the weak-side block. 1 shoots or looks for 4 or 5 low (figure 3).

Points of Emphasis

In an elevator screen two players stand next to each other with slight space between them. The idea is to allow a teammate through the opening but then to close the space before the defender passes through, like an elevator door closing and leaving a would-be passenger outside. The primary scoring opportunity is for 2 with a 15- to 20-foot (4.5-6 m) shot off the elevator screen.

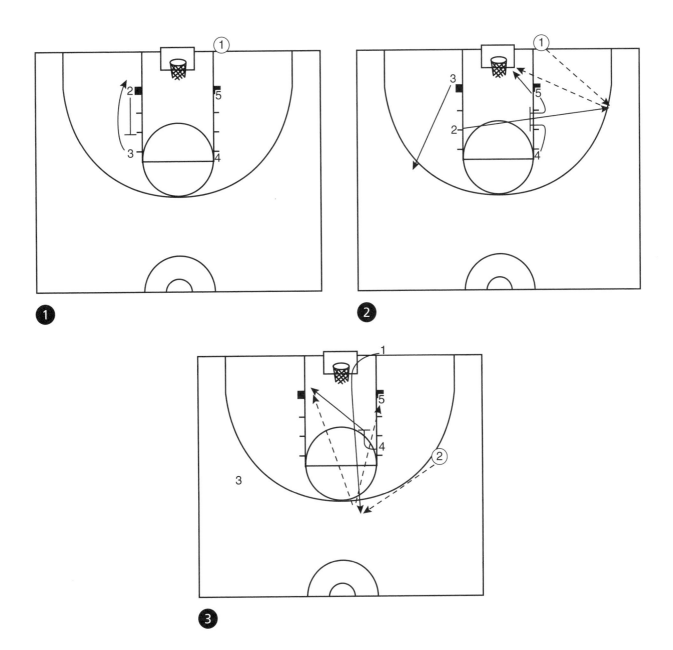

SQUARE 2

Beth Burns

Objectives

- To provide multiple scoring options on the baseline out-of-bounds play.
- To position a shooter in a different starting spot on the floor or to use her as a decoy.
- To safely inbound the ball.

When to Use

Against a man-to-man defense.

Key Personnel

Your 1 should be a precision passer who can shoot the three. Your 2 is your biggest guard, able to finish in traffic. Your 3 is your best perimeter shooter. Your 4 needs to be a great screener with ability to score off the duck-in. Your 5 is your best low-post scorer, able to catch and finish in traffic, and a good screener.

Execution

1. On the ball slap, 2 up-screens 3, who cuts to the weak-side block (figure 1).
2. 2 slips through an elevator screen by 4 and 5 to curl around 5 to the basket, where 1 feeds her if she's open. If not, 2 continues to the weak-side corner as 3 slips through the elevator screen to receive the pass for a 15- to 20-foot (4.5-6 m) shot (figure 2).
3. If 3 doesn't shoot, she passes to 1, who has flashed up the lane to the top of the key off 4's screen. 4 continues from the screen to the weak-side block. 1 shoots or looks for 4 or 5 low (figure 3).

Points of Emphasis

The success of this play begins with the up screen from 2, who needs to set a good screen for 3 and then release into the elevator screen. 2 may look for a shot but generally serves as the decoy running through the first elevator screen. 3 is most likely to receive an open shot in the second elevator screen.

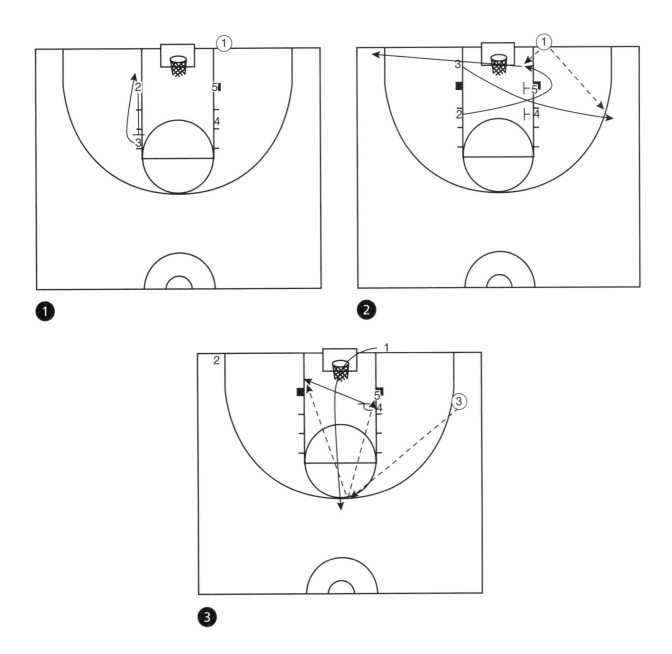

SQUARE 3

Beth Burns

Objectives

- To give a post player and perimeter player a scoring option.
- To safely inbound the ball.

When to Use

- In short-second situations against either a man to man or zone (works best against man to man).
- For multiple offensive scoring opportunities.
- After using Square 1 a few times.

Key Personnel

Your 1 should be a precision passer who can shoot the three. Your 2 must be able to hit a perimeter shot off the catch-and-shoot and set a back screen. Your 3 should be a good three-point shooter who can stretch the defense and shoot from the corner. Your 4 needs to be a good athlete with size who can catch and finish on the block. Your 5 should be a good screener and low-block scorer.

Execution

1. On the ball slap, 2 diagonal-screens 4, who cuts to the weak-side block looking for the feed from 1. 3 opens to the weak-side corner (figure 1).
2. 5 screens 2, who heads to the ball-side corner for the pass from 1. 1 runs to the top of the key through the lane (figure 2).
3. 2 passes back to 1, who looks at 5 flashing in the lane and 4 either flashing in the lane or up the lane to above the arc (figure 3).

Points of Emphasis

It's very important for 2 to set a quick up screen for 4, who will get a good scoring opportunity with a well-set screen. If 2 sets a good screen, this makes her defender help on the cutting 4 and thus allows 2 to go off a screen from 5.

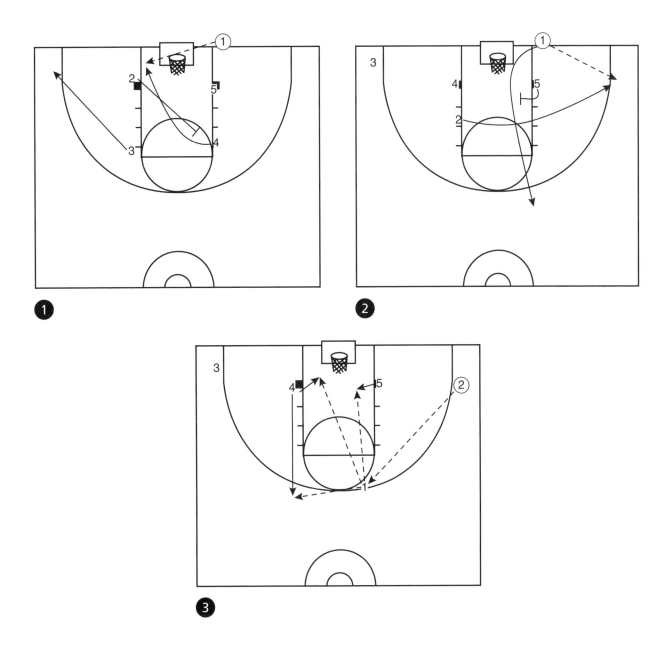

BASELINE UP

Beth Burns

Objective

To provide a low-post scoring opportunity via the baseline inbounds play.

When to Use

- Against a man-to-man defense.
- As a continuation into a flex offense.
- In short-second situations.

Key Personnel

Your 1 needs to be a good lob passer and a great screener. Your 2 should be able to pass to the low block with either hand. Your 3 needs to be proficient from behind the arc to spread the defense. Your 4 is your best low-post scorer who can come off a flex screen to score in the key. Your 5 must create a passing angle over the top, catch, and deliver the ball elbow to elbow.

Execution

1. On the ball slap, 5 cuts up the lane to receive the pass. 2 waits until the ball is in the air to cut up the lane (figure 1).
2. 1 jumps in and sets a flex screen for 4, who flashes to the opposite block. 5 passes to 4 if she's open. If not, 5 feeds 2, who feeds 4. 3 starts toward the wing before crashing the boards (figure 2).

Points of Emphasis

A flex screen is a screen on the block used usually by a guard on a cut from the baseline wing. The post player sits on the block, and the guard cuts right on top of the screen to the front of the rim, allowing her to get a layup.

The 2 and 5 players need to be good decoys and cut hard to the top of the key to allow 1 to step in and set a good flex screen on 4's defender. With the defenders on 2 and 4 high, space is created in the paint for 4 to cut over 1 and receive a pass next to an open basket.

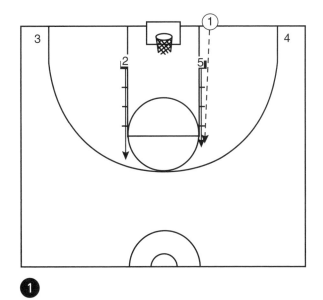

1

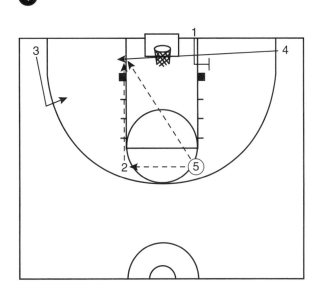

2

SIDE 2

Lisa Stone

Objective

To get a quick score.

When to Use

- When the ball is placed near the timeline or free-throw line area of the court and the offense is looking for a quick attacking play.
- Against a man-to-man defense.

Key Personnel

Your 3 must be able to set solid screens. Your 2 must be a decisive and good passer who is also a great shooter with ability to read screens and hunt a shot.

Execution

1. 5 sets a cross-screen for 1. 3 immediately sets a back-screen for 5 cutting to the basket to receive a lob pass from 2 (figure 1).
2. Should the pass not be open, 2 passes to 1, steps inbounds, and reads the defense to decide whether to use 4's screen at the bottom of the lane for a shot at the bucket or a stagger screen by 3 and 5 to roll back up to the top of the key for a three-pointer (figure 2).

Variation

The 2 and 4 can employ a pick-and-roll if 4 screens 2 on the shallow wing (figure 3).

Point of Emphasis

The 2 must read the defense well, from the initial inbounds pass to finding her shot off an assortment of screens.

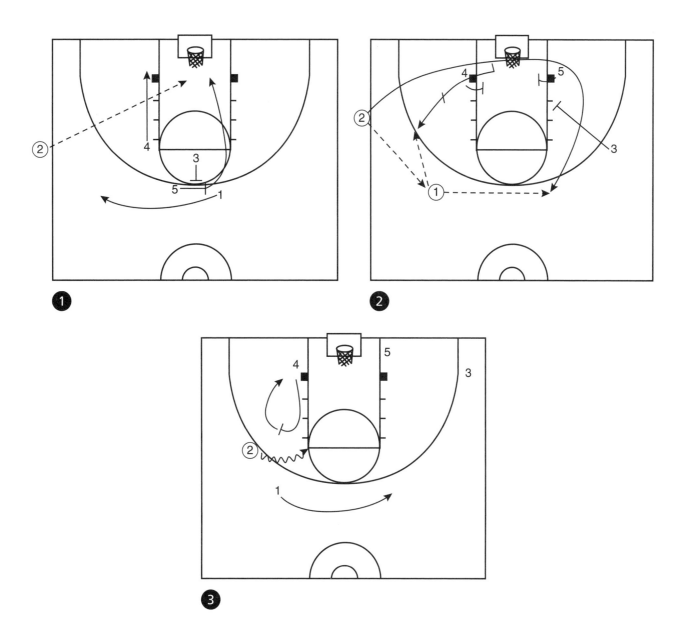

Beating the Press

When an opponent presses, this doesn't mean they automatically dictate ball movement or game tempo. A well-coached offensive team should have plenty of ways to offset the pressure that a full-court defense can create.

Opponents might choose to press for a number of reasons: as a late-game tactic when trailing, when outmatched in the half-court game, when they possess a significant speed advantage, when facing a team with subpar ball handlers, or when they want to disrupt the flow of an offense. These are just a few of the many reasons for choosing the full-court press. But no matter the reason the defense has for choosing to press, an offense can often create an advantage against the press and dissuade the defense from further pressing. The offense achieves this through carefully designed plays that consider a team's personnel and skill set, and by coaching players to successfully execute the press break. After all, if a team repeatedly gets beat while pressing, it doesn't make sense to continue doing so.

When breaking a press, there are two possible objectives. The aggressive objective is to beat the other team down the court with the ball and take a high-percentage shot in a 2-on-1 or 3-on-2 situation. The safer option is simply to get the ball up the floor in order to run a half-court offense. The game situation and team personnel will dictate which plan makes the most sense.

Imparting a few principles when teaching a team to break a press can have a huge impact on the team's ability to make sound decisions. Teach players to inbound the ball quickly to give the defense little time to set up and run their press. Encourage them to move the ball up the floor quickly to negate the trapping nature of presses—a slow-moving ball is a press's dream. They should avoid sidelines, especially near the baseline and just beyond half-court because those areas make trapping much easier. Given that speed is an asset, players should look to pass first and dribble second. Train them to come back to meet a pass rather than waiting for the ball to arrive and to spread the floor to make the defense work harder. The middle of most zone presses are vulnerable, so put a post player with good hands there to provide a big, reliable target. Keep a player behind the ball as a safety valve in case the ball handler gets into trouble.

Putting the right players in the right positions can be the difference in successfully breaking a press and repeatedly turning the ball over. The inbounds player must have great passing and decision-making skills. Your best ball handler should have the ball in her hands as much as possible unless, in a late-game situation, your best free-throw shooter doesn't present a significant drop-off in ball-handling skills. In this case, she should handle the ball to maximize the opportunity to score if fouled.

Perhaps the skill most important in beating a press is maintaining composure. Far too many well-in-hand games have been lost when a desperate opponent springs a full-court press and converts on a few turnovers within seconds against players who have lost their cool. Often a deep breath to clear the head and counter the frenzy a press brings allows an offense to regain control.

PRESS BREAK 1-4 LOW

Felisha Legette-Jack

Objective

To break a full-court, man-to-man press.

When to Use

Against a full-court, man-to-man press.

Key Personnel

Your 4 player should be a smart inbounder who makes good decisions with the ball. Your 1 player is your most reliable ball handler.

Execution

1 flashes to the sideline while 3, 2, and 5 release long. 4 throws to whoever is open. If 1 receives the ball, 2, 3, and 5 vacate the area to relieve defensive pressure, and 4 may set a screen to help 1 get into the open court. 1 dribbles up the floor (see the figure).

Points of Emphasis

This play is effective because of the simultaneous action and movement of all the players. The 1 must time her flash to the ball to be open to receive it. She must take care to catch the ball before turning up the court. The 4 must make a good decision of whom to inbound to and must throw a strike to a streaking player if one is open.

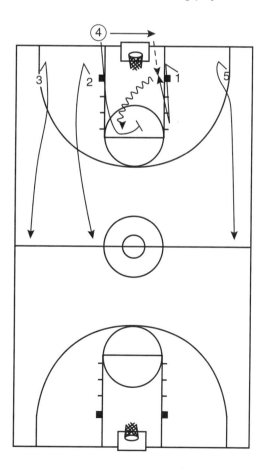

PRESS BREAK 4-3

Felisha Legette-Jack

Objective

To break a full- or three-quarter-court zone press.

When to Use

Against a full- or three-quarter-court zone press.

Key Personnel

Your 3 player should have good hands, be an effective dribbler, and make good decisions with the ball.

Execution

1. 1 flashes toward the strong-side corner while 2 cuts toward the weak-side corner. 4 throws to either 1 or 2. If 1 catches the ball, 3 flashes middle from the weak side and receives the ball while 2 runs the sideline (figure 1).

2. 4 replaces 2 as the safety. 3 looks opposite for 2 running downcourt. If 2 is not open, she can attack the basket using the dribble or reverse the ball to 4. If she passes to 4, 5 continues to occupy the middle, looking for the ball back to advance it (figure 2).

Points of Emphasis

The timing of 3's flash from the weak side should neither make her late or cause her to wait for the ball. She must focus on catching the ball before looking upcourt.

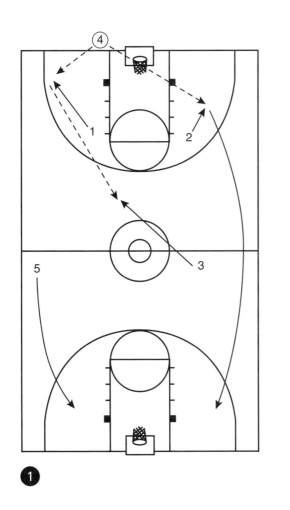

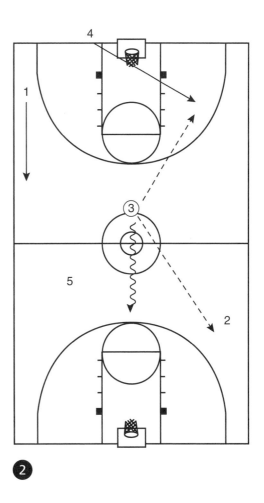

PRESS BREAK 4-5

Felisha Legette-Jack

Objective

To break a full- or three-quarter-court zone press.

When to Use

Against a full- or three-quarter-court zone press.

Key Personnel

Your 5 player must have good hands, be able to dribble effectively, and make good decisions with the ball. Your 1 player should be skilled in ballhandling, passing, and decision making.

Execution

1. 1 flashes toward the strong-side corner as 2 cuts toward the baseline. 4 throws to 1 or 2. If 1 receives the ball, 5 flashes middle from the weak side and 2 runs the sideline (figure 1).
2. 4 replaces 2 and serves as a safety. 1 passes to 5, who catches and looks for 2 running down the court. If 2 is not open, 5 reverses the ball to 4 and continues occupying the middle (figure 2).

Points of Emphasis

This play is effective because the middle of most zone presses is most vulnerable, and putting a post player there makes for a big target and relieves some pressure. Timing and personnel are key. The 5's flash from the weak side must happen neither late nor make her wait for the ball. She must focus on catching the ball before looking upcourt.

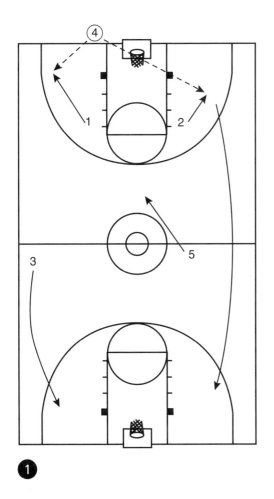

1

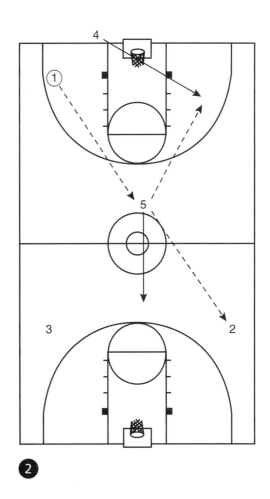

2

ARKANSAS SPECIAL

Matthew Mitchell

Objective

To get the ball inbounds and into the hands of the best free-throw shooter.

When to Use

- In late game situations after a made basket against full-court, man-to-man pressure when an immediate foul is expected.
- Best used after running Arkansas (see p. 220).

Key Personnel

Your 1 and 2 should be your best free-throw shooters.

Execution

1. When the referee hands the ball to 1, 2 sprints out of bounds to receive the pass. 3, 4, and 5 sprint downcourt to pull the defense away from the ball (figure 1).
2. 1 steps inbounds to receive the pass from 2 (figure 2).

Points of Emphasis

This play is a good counter to teams who have already seen the Arkansas during the game. The 1 and 2 must be good free-throw shooters who can handle the ball and make good decisions under pressure.

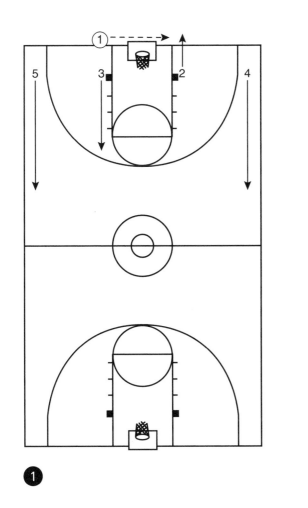

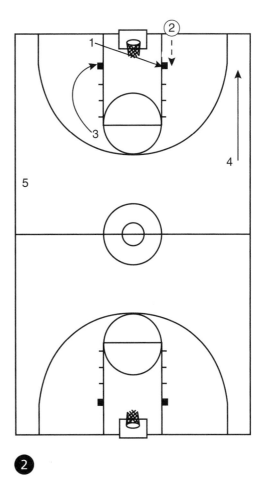

DIAMOND

Matthew Mitchell

Objectives

- To advance the ball in pressure situations.
- To put the ball in the hands of the best free-throw shooter on the initial pass when the defense needs a quick foul.

When to Use

- Against a denial man-to-man, full-court press.
- When a basket is needed in a late-game situation.

Key Personnel

Your 2 should be your best free-throw shooter. Your 5 must be able to catch and dribble on the run without turning the ball over.

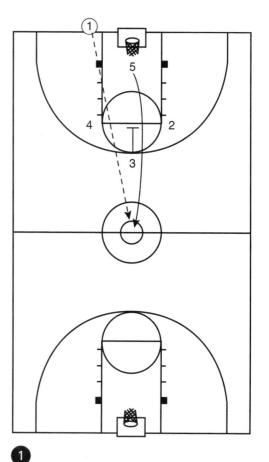

Execution

1. 3 sets a back screen for 5. 1 looks upcourt for the long pass, especially in late-game situations when the defense is fronting (figure 1).

2. 3 and 4 set a stagger screen for 2, who cuts hard to the free-throw line extended or above to receive the pass. 3 and 4 roll back to the ball. 1 passes to 2 and then steps inbounds as a pressure release (figure 2).

3. 3 flashes to the middle of the floor as 4 cuts to the ball-side sideline. 2 advances the ball by dribbling or passing to 3 or 4, or kicks it back to 1 (figure 3).

Points of Emphasis

This plays provides several options for getting the ball inbounds. The post-to-guard screen makes it difficult for the defense to be in complete denial because defenders must either switch or trail the screen.

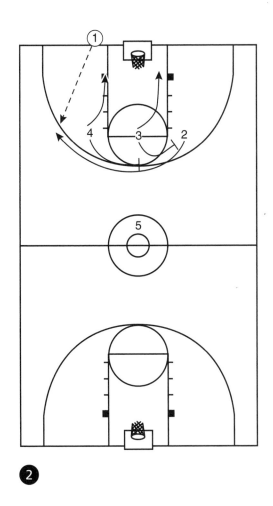

2

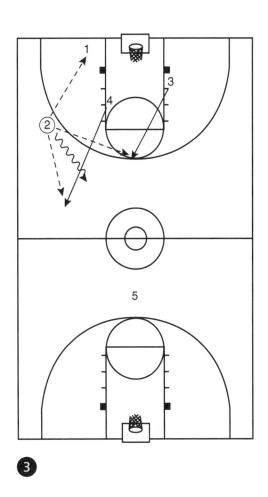

3

REGULAR

Matthew Mitchell

Objective

To spread the floor and advance the ball via passing or dribbling.

When to Use

Against a full-court man-to-man or zone press.

Key Personnel

Your 1 must be a good decision-maker, dribbler, and passer. Your 1 and 2 should be the fastest players on the court. Your 2 must recognize and fill open areas.

Execution

1. 2 screens for 1, who cuts to the ball. 2 rolls back to the ball. 4 passes to 1 as 3 cuts to the ball-side sideline near half-court (figure 1).

2. 1 can either dribble or look to 2 flashing into the middle of the defense, and then to 3 on the sideline, and then back to 4 (figure 2).

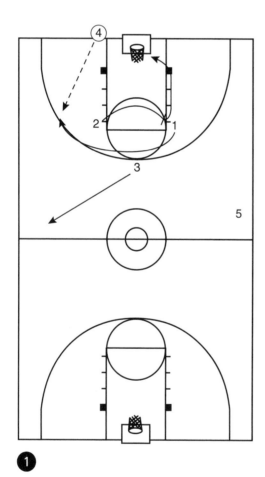

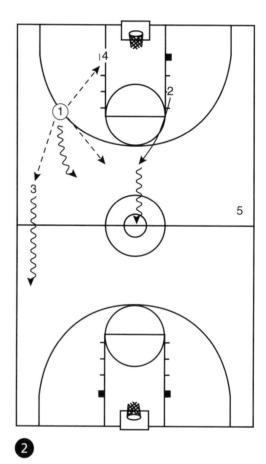

218

3. If 4 receives the ball, 5 flashes toward the baseline for the pass (figure 3).
4. 5 then passes to 2 flashing to the sideline or to 1 flashing to the middle of the court (figure 4).

Variation

If 1 is being defended tightly, 4 sprints ahead and sets a screen in the backcourt to relieve the pressure.

Points of Emphasis

If used against zone pressure, 1 must have options to advance the ball up the sideline or the middle of the court and know that passing back to 4 is an acceptable option. If used against man-to-man pressure, everyone should clear out of the backcourt once 1 has the ball so she can take the defender one on one up the floor.

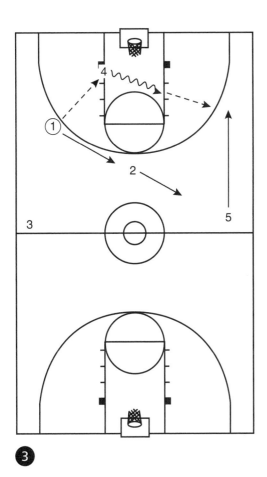

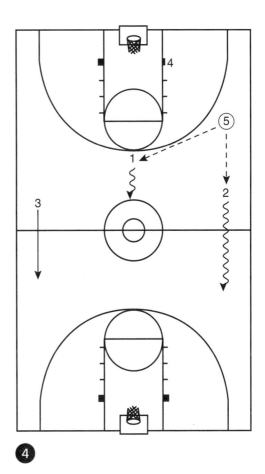

ARKANSAS

Matthew Mitchell

Objective

To get the ball in the hands of the best free-throw shooter or ball handler.

When to Use

- In late-game situations.
- Against a full-court man-to-man press, especially if the defense is trapping on the initial inbounds pass.

Key Personnel

Your 1 must make quick decisions and be accurate with short and long passes. Your 2 is your best free-throw shooter and your 3 your best ball handler.

Execution

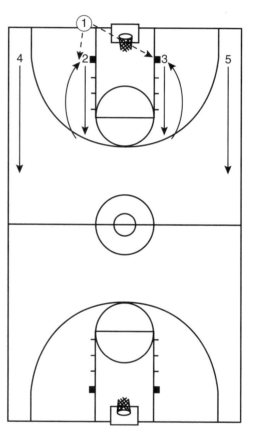

When the referee hands the ball to 1, the other four players turn and sprint downcourt. 2 and 3 cut back to the ball while 4 and 5 sprint past half-court to clear out the defense for any potential traps. 1 passes to 2 or 3, then steps inbounds and stays behind the ball as a pressure release (figure 1).

Points of Emphasis

This press offense challenges the opponent to choose how to defend. If the defense fronts or denies, the long pass to 4 or 5 is open. If the defense plays behind, 2 or 3 will be open. It's very important that all players sprint down the court and that your best free-throw shooter and ball handler cut hard back to the ball. The 4 and 5 must sprint hard downcourt to force the defense to commit to them.

Quick-Shot Plays

You're down by 1 with the ball at midcourt and nine seconds on the clock. The championship is on the line. Your shooting guard has the hot hand, but the opponent's post has fouled out. What play do you call?

The shot clock is approaching single digits. Your team is up by 2 midway through the third quarter of a tight playoff game. Your offense has been out of rhythm all second half. What play do you call?

Your opponent has just scored to go up by 3 with eight seconds remaining in the game. Your best perimeter shooter has fouled out. What play do you call?

These scenarios, or similar ones, play out night after night in gymnasiums and arenas across the country. The only objective is getting the ball in the player's hands who has the best chance of scoring the necessary points, whether that means drawing a foul and going to the free-throw line, scoring a two-pointer, or sinking a three.

The difference between a successful end to a game and an unsuccessful one often doesn't hinge solely on the play called. As time ticks down with the game on the line, execution and poise will usually get the win. Frenzy and sloppiness more often get the loss. Under pressure, players must narrow their focus to executing the play exactly as it's drawn up, using honed fundamentals while staying flexible and level-headed enough to ad-lib if necessary. They must understand—and have been coached—how long (and short) a few seconds can be.

Coaches must display the calm they want to see in their players. While maintaining their composure, they need to feed their players the exact information they need to know—no more, no less. Several pieces of information might be vital, including how much time is remaining on the game clock and shot clock, how many points are needed in that possession, how many time-outs they have and if they should use one if they get in trouble, who is in foul trouble from both teams, the team bonus situation for both teams, and how aggressive to be. A defense nursing a lead tends to play softer, so driving to the basket can lead either to a foul or a relatively easy basket. Being overly aggressive can lead to a game-losing turnover.

To make the best play call, a coach should also consider who has the hot hands and who has the iciest veins, how effective the offense and defense have been thus far in the game, and how much time the play takes to set up and run from both live and dead-ball situations. With under two seconds on the clock, catching and shooting is really the only legitimate option unless the defense inexplicably gives the receiver room for one clear dribble to the basket. Three to five seconds is enough time for a dribble or two, but a pass is not recommended because there's too much danger of a turnover or mishandled pass. Five to 10 seconds is enough time for a dribble or two and a pass, or maybe a couple of passes.

The plays in this chapter provide many options to score quickly in a variety of situations—as long as all players are well versed in their execution, have practiced last-second situations, and understand the importance of fundamentals and poise.

PUSH

Tia Jackson

Objective

To get the best three-point shooter a shot within six seconds.

When to Use

- As a quick-hitter against a man-to-man defense.
- At the end of the half, game, or shot clock.
- As a quick three-pointer on an inbounds situation on the opposite baseline.

Key Personnel

Your 3 is your best shooter or a player with a hot hand. Your 5 is your strongest low-post player. Your 4 is one of your best screeners, ideally with three-point range as well.

Execution

4 inbounds to 1 and trails behind as 1 drives up the right side of the court, pushing 3 off the wing. 3 runs off a screen by 5, who then posts up. If 5's defender helps with 3, 1 passes to 5. 4 sets a screen for 3 just below the free-throw line. 3 comes hard off both screens, looking for a shot (see the figure).

Variations

- If only a two-pointer is needed, one variation is to clear out for 1 to take the ball coast to coast at the end of the game, possibly using a blind screen by 5.
- In another variation 4 sets a flare screen instead of a down screen for 3 so 3 can get behind the arc for a three-pointer.

Points of Emphasis

This play will work only if 4 headhunts 3's defender and sets a solid screen. The 5 must post up big after setting her screen if the play is run for 2 or 3.

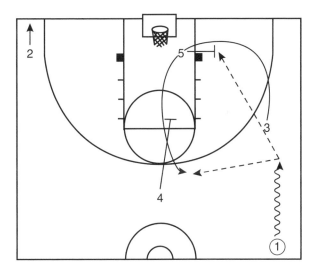

DOUBLE FLARE

Tia Jackson

Objective

To get a hot hand a three-pointer, an isolation for a baseline drive, or a lob over the top.

When to Use

As the clock is winding down.

Key Personnel

Your 2 must be a threat to shoot or drive and able to handle a lob pass on the back side. Your 4 and 5 must work well together in setting two quick double screens.

Execution

1. 1 dribbles right, appearing to attack, as 5 crosses the key to set a double screen with 4 for 3. 3 cuts through the baseline as a decoy. 2 pretends to cut backdoor on the strong side but then flares above the free-throw line off a double screen by 4 and 5. 1 passes to 2, who looks to shoot (figure 1).

2. If 2's defender stays with her, she looks for the one-on-one drive to the baseline, kicking the ball out to 3 if she draws the weak-side defender. If 2's defender chases her over the top of the flare screen by 4 and 5, 2 lobs to 5 for the alley-oop (figure 2).

Variation

If either post defender steps up to help 2's defender, that post should slip to the basket.

Points of Emphasis

The play takes about 10 seconds to execute. Your 2 player should practice her footwork for running off a flare for the catch-and-shoot because this doesn't come naturally to most players. The 3 must cut hard to take her defender with her.

1

2

3

Van Chancellor

Objectives

- To create a perimeter-to-post screening situation that makes it difficult for the defense to switch.
- To help a perimeter player get open.

When to Use

- To isolate a post player for a touch inside.
- As a quick hitter.
- As an entry to motion or a continuity set.

Key Personnel

For the variation, the 2 player needs good skills at the post. The 1 should be a solid ball-handling point guard.

Execution

1. 1 dribbles to the wing. 2 sets a back screen for 5, who cuts hard to the strong-side block for a possible feed and shot (figure 1).
2. 4 down-screens for 2, who pops for a possible shot on a pass from 1 (figure 2).
3. After 2 receives the ball, 4 comes up to set a ball screen for her. 2 drives around the screen while 3 flattens out to the corner (figure 3).

Variation

If 2 has some size or good posting skills, she can drop as if going to screen for 5 and then reverse back and post up her defender (figure 4).

Points of Emphasis

The entire play shouldn't take more than 10 seconds. Timing is important. The 2 must not set the screen for 5 before 1 gets to the wing with the ball. Otherwise the defense has time to recover and defend the play. The ability to make a proper low-post feed is imperative. Screens must be set at the correct angle, and the cutter must cut hard and tight off the screen.

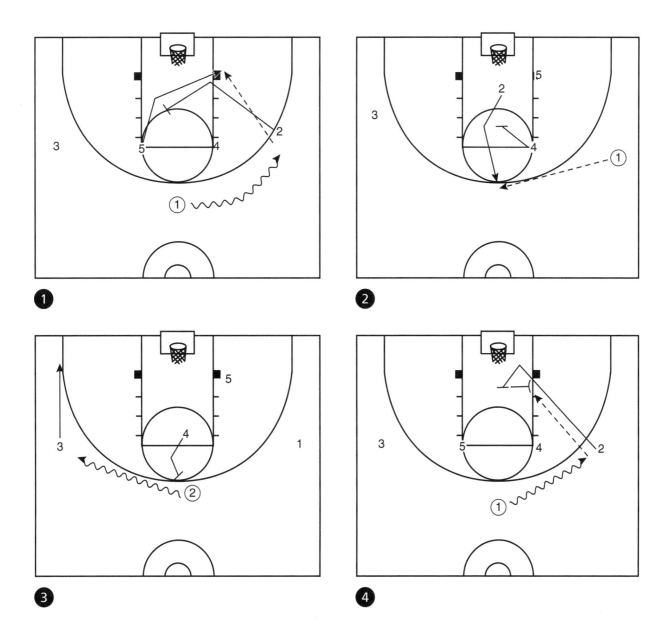

C

Van Chancellor

Objective

To force a post defender to match up against a dribbling guard on the perimeter or to leave her open for a shot behind a screen.

When to Use

- Against a team that does not defend the ball screen well.
- When certain matchups are advantageous, such as when 2 is guarded by a poor ball defender who struggles to navigate ball screens.
- With a special offensive player talented in making decisions off the dribble.

Key Personnel

Your 2 player must handle the ball well and make the proper read coming off a ball screen. Your 4 must screen well and be either a strong, inside player who can roll to the basket after screening or a small forward who can pop out for a perimeter shot after screening.

Execution

1. 1 passes to 2 and then rubs off 4. If 1 is open off the screen, 2 can feed 1 near the basket for a close-range shot. If 1 doesn't receive the ball, she continues to the opposite corner (figure 1).
2. 4 then sets a ball screen for 2, who comes off hard, looking to attack the paint. If the defense traps, 2 uses a back-out dribble and hits 4 rolling to the basket. If the defense goes behind the screen, 2 shoots. If the defense takes away the shot and pass to 4, 5 steps across the lane for a possible feed (figure 2).

Variation

Many times the defense will choose to trap the ball screen or at least give a hard hedge, step out, and block the dribbler's path. In these situations, if 4 sees the defender on her outside shoulder, she slips the screen (figure 3).

Points of Emphasis

There are no small details. Each cut and pass must be exactly right to put each player on the floor in the right position. The 2 shouldn't step so far away from the basket to catch the initial entry pass that the ball screen becomes ineffective. She should catch the ball and assume the triple-threat position. The 4 should sprint to screen and be aggressive in her position. The 1 should attack the screen while also reading the defender.

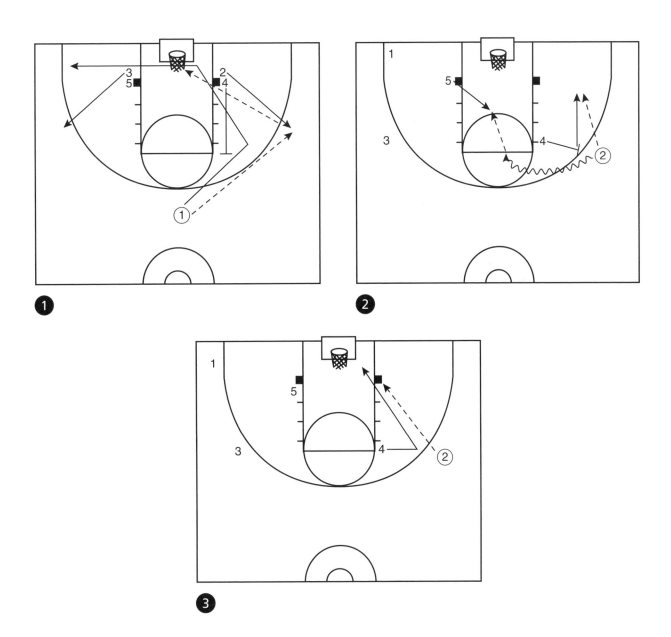

FIST

Van Chancellor

Objectives

- To pressure a team by putting their defenders in the uncomfortable position of defending the live dribble in the open space of the top of the key.
- To create room for a talented point guard.

When to Use

- In transition as the point guard is advancing the ball down the floor.
- As a half-court entry to create a shot or flow into another offense.
- As the shot clock is running down.

Key Personnel

Your 1 player requires some speed and quickness with the dribble and must make good decisions off the dribble.

Execution

1. 1 dribble-entries off-center with her dominant hand to the outside of a ball screen by 4 at the top of the key. 1 feeds 4 who's popping to an open area ready for a jump shot if the defense traps or hedges on the screen (figure 1).
2. If 4 isn't open, 5 sets another ball screen for 1 and then rolls to the rim. If the defense traps or hedges, 5 might be open for a layup. At the same time, 4 pops back up so that if her defender helps on 5 cutting to the rim, 4 will have an open jumper (figure 2).

Variation

Screening the screener can yield an open look for a good shooter. The 2 sets a ball screen for 1 at the top of the key, and then 5 sets an elbow screen for 2 (figure 3). If 2's defender helps on the ball screen, it will be difficult for her to get over the elbow screen.

Points of Emphasis

The play should take only about five seconds to execute. Floor spacing among all five players must be good to allow room for the ball handler to attack. The 4 must set the screen and not move to avoid an offensive foul. The 1 must attack the screener and drive the ball off the screen, not allowing space for her defender to slide through.

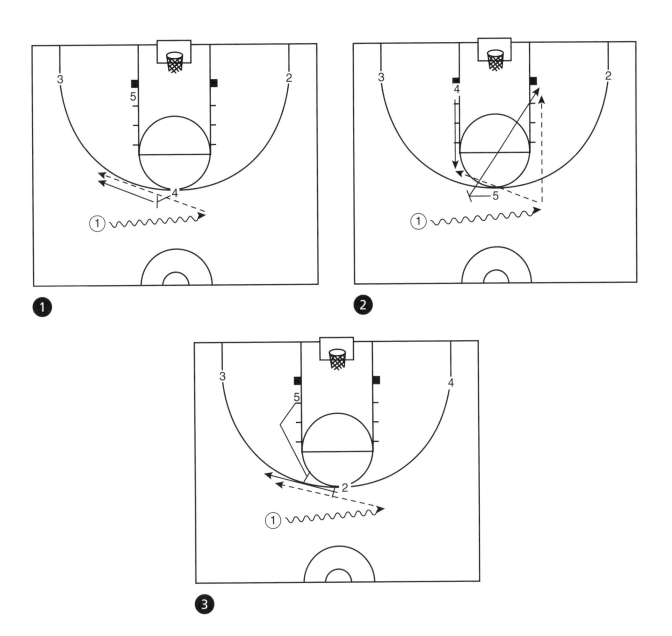

REGGIE MILLER

Van Chancellor

Objectives

- To put pressure on the defender guarding the scorer by forcing her to fight through several screens.
- To get an average shooter but above-average driver a good touch.

When to Use

- Out of a time-out or to start the half.
- When your best scorer needs to get involved.

Key Personnel

Your 2 must be able to shoot or drive off the catch. Your 1 should be able to handle the ball and deliver it to the cutter at precisely the right time.

Execution

1. In this setup, 2 is the primary scorer. 1 dribbles toward 2 but then reverses to the other side. 2 runs the baseline off a triple stagger screen by 4 on the weak side of the lane, 3 in the middle of the lane, and 5 on the strong side. 1 passes to 2 for a jump shot (figure 1).
2. If 2 doesn't shoot, 5 sets a ball screen for 2, who drives and creates. (figure 2).

Variation

One of the most effective variations of this play is 2 curling off the third screen (figure 3). Most defenders will tag this cut, meaning they'll trail the cutter on her back side. When 2 curls, 5 pin-screens for 3, who's often the best option.

Points of Emphasis

The initial baseline run should take only a few seconds off the clock. It's important that 3 gets to the middle of the lane to set the second screen. If she sets the third and last screen, this allows the defense an easy opportunity to switch. The 2 must cut hard and tight against the screens to ensure the best possibility of getting open. The screens must be solid and at the right angle; screeners, once in position, must be still and let 2 do the work. The point guard reads if the cutter is flaring or curling and delivers the ball at the right time.

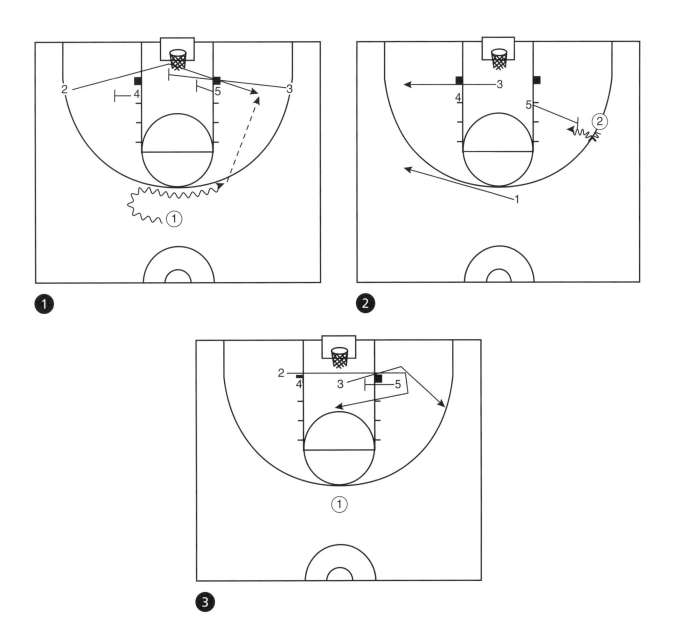

TRIPLE

Van Chancellor

Objectives

- To distort the defense and create space for a post feed.
- To pressure the defense with many offensive possibilities.
- To isolate a post for a touch inside.

When to Use

As an entry into motion or other continuity offense.

Key Personnel

You need a player who can post inside—either a post player or a perimeter player with height advantage. The players in the stack should be able to shoot or drive, or both. Your 4 should be able to shoot to stretch the defense.

Execution

1. 2 pops out to the wing or the corner from the bottom of the stack, and 3 fills the other position. 1 passes to 2, who might find 5 open. 1 then runs off an elbow screen by 4 to the weak-side wing, primarily to occupy the help-side defense for a clean post feed (figure 1).
2. If the defense helps on 1, 4 flashes to the ball-side high post for a pass from 2 and then hits 5 stepping across the lane (figure 2). If nothing is available, move into a continuity offense.

Variations

- First, 2 can curl off of the top of the stack for a possible feed inside the lane (figure 3).
- Second, 1 can dribble to the wing. 2 steps inside the screen and moves up the lane, looking for a ball screen from 4 and the pass from 1 (figure 4).
- Third, 1 can dribble to the wing away from the stack off a ball screen by 4, who pops for a possible shot (figure 5).

Points of Emphasis

This play should take no more than five seconds off the clock. By lining up players in a triple stack, you give the defense a look it rarely sees. It's important that everyone understands each player's strengths. This is a great entry for a great low-post player, in which case you should set the stack on the player's go-to side. Or a great perimeter player can work with an average post player off the curl or ball-screen option. The secondary movement can be designed to fit your personnel or how you want to attack the defense. The point guard must be able to make the proper read and deliver the ball to the right player at the right time.

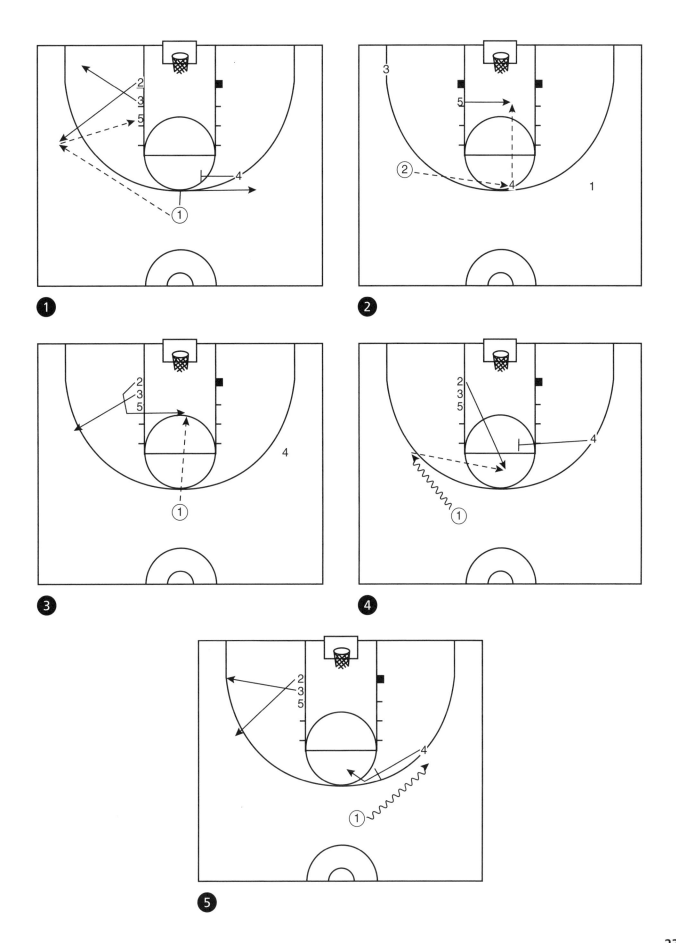

1

2

3

4

5

DUCK-IN

Maria Fantanarosa

Objectives

- To create scoring opportunities for four players using 12 seconds or less of the clock.
- To create high-percentage scoring opportunities for back-to-basket players, taking little time off the shot clock.
- To allow guards to attack the basket, creating free-throw opportunities.

When to Use

- As a quick hit or continuity offense.
- Against either man-to-man or zone defenses.

Key Personnel

Your 1 must be a good decision-maker and scorer. Your 4 and 5 should be versatile enough to score facing the basket or with their backs to the basket. Your 2 and 3 should be able to hit the three.

Execution

1. As 1 advances across midcourt, 2 and 3 come off down screens by 4 and 5 and pop out to the tight wing areas (figure 1).
2. 4 and 5 open to the middle, giving 1 immediate options in the paint. 1 dribbles to the right side as 2 drops to the corner (figure 2).
3. 5 sets a midangle ball screen for 1. 1 looks to drive or shoot as 5 slips, rolls, or pops, ready for a pass if 1 is trapped. Meanwhile, as another option, 4 ducks into and out of the lane in the midpost area. 1 passes to 3, who is spotted up for a three-pointer (figure 3).
4. 4 drop-seals in the paint as 1 follows behind to the strong-side baseline. 5 drops to the weak-side block as 2 pops above the three-point line (figure 4).
5. 4 sets a midangle ball screen for 3, who looks to drive or shoot, and the play turns into a continuity offense (figure 5).

Variations

- If opponents trap the ball screens, 1 may slip by 5 before the screen is set to get 5's defender out of the way before attacking. If 4 is guarded by a larger defender, she should set the first ball screen to bring the "big" out.
- If 4's defender is cheating to the high side, anticipating the duck, 4 flashes to the strong-side low block as 5 moves up the lane to set the ball screen.
- If the defenders on the guards begin anticipating the ball screen, 1 should pass to 2 or 3 and float to the weak side to allow for a baseline rip.

Points of Emphasis

This play is hard to stop if you have a dominant back-to-the-basket scorer and consistent three-point shooters, but timing and spacing are important. The 2 and 3 should start rim front, and their L-cuts off the down screens must be tight. This way, if the defense hedges the ball screen, the guard can attack on the dribble and decrease the passing lane to both the duck-in post and weak-side wing. The duck-in post must begin to set up the duck as the guard reaches the shoulder of the ball screen. After passing to 3, 1 sprints behind the duck-in post and gets through to the baseline to be an option if the defense cheats to guard the rolling post. Otherwise, she and her defender crowd the area and take away that option.

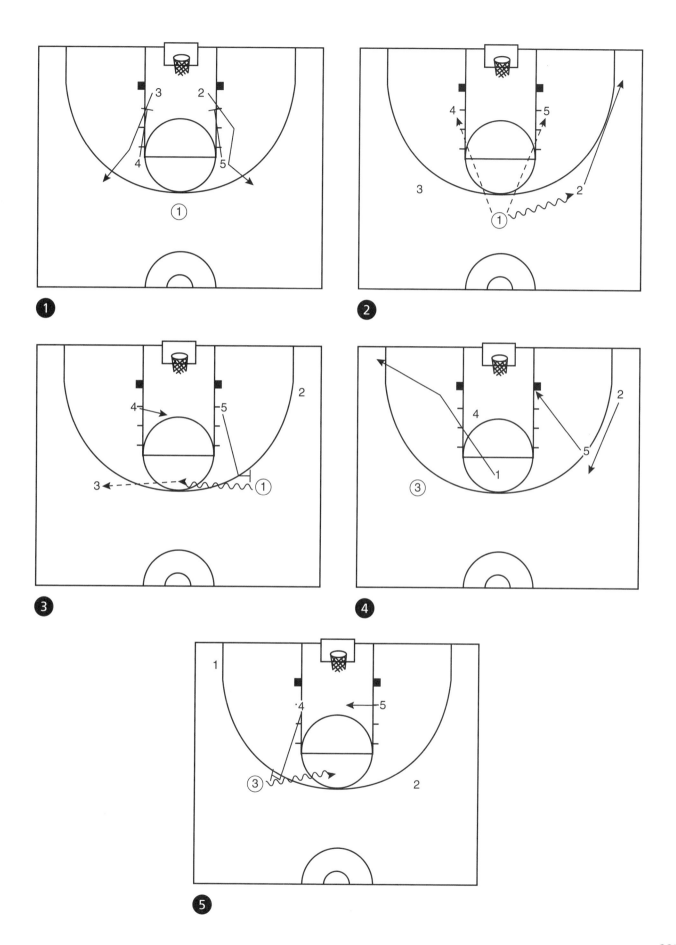

FLARE AND DIVE

Maria Fantanarosa

Objective

To get the point guard a three-point look or give the post a high-percentage scoring opportunity in the paint.

When to Use

- As a half-court inbounds play against a man-to-man defense when the defense sags off a point guard with three-point range.
- When post defenders help too long on screens.

Key Personnel

Your 5 should be a good passer, and your 1 must have three-point range. Your 2 should slash well to the hoop. Your 3 should be a threat from behind the arc.

Execution

1. 1 passes to 5, and 3 immediately clears out to the right baseline. 4 sets a flare screen for 1 and then dives to the weak-side block (figure 1).
2. 5 passes back to 1, now on the left wing. 2 slashes to the strong-side low block as 4 and 5 set a stagger screen for 3 curling to the top of the key (figure 2).

Variation

If the defender starts to chase over the top of the flare screen, 4 switches to a back screen and 1 cuts backdoor for a pass from 5. If 5 passes to 4, 4 pops up for a three-point look instead of diving to the basket (figure 3).

Points of Emphasis

This play takes 10 to 12 seconds to execute. The 3 must clear immediately as the ball is entered to 5. The 1 leaves no space between her and the screen. If the flare is not open, 1 goes hard backdoor. If she doesn't receive the pass, this movement helps her get open for the reversal and allows the play to continue.

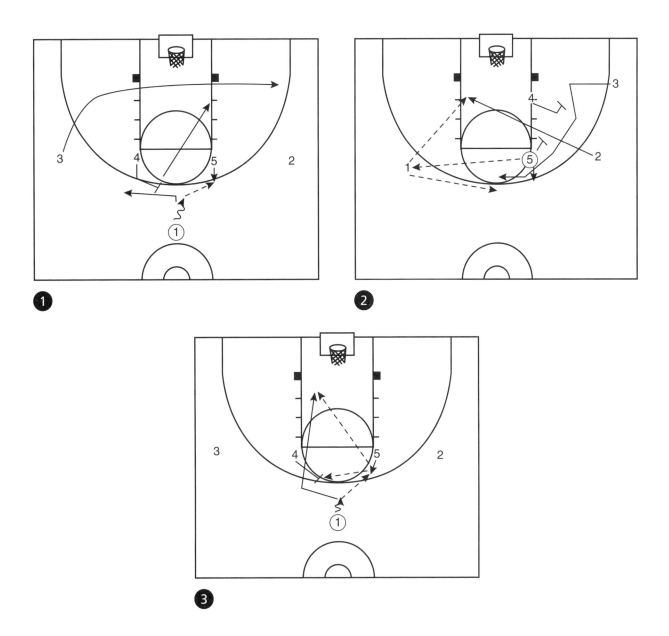

JUMP SHOT BETTY

Maria Fantanarosa

Objective

To give a point guard several scoring opportunities in the same quick hitter.

When to Use

As a half-court inbounds play against a man-to-man defense.

Key Personnel

1 must be a scorer. 3 penetrates well. 4 and 5 have good fundamentals and are able to screen, pass, and threaten with the ball.

Execution

1. 1 passes to either 4 or 5 on the elbow, in this case 4. 5 sets a back screen for 1, who flashes down to the weak-side block (figure 1).

2. 4 passes to 3. 4 and 5 immediately down-screen for 1, who pops to the top of the key. 3 shoots, creates off the dribble, or passes to 1. 4 seals in the post for another option (figure 2).

Variation

If the defense starts to switch on the back screen, 5 dives to the strong-side low block to take advantage of the mismatch with 1's defender (figure 3).

Points of Emphasis

This play takes 10 to 12 seconds to execute. The 1 must rub shoulders with both screeners. The down screen occurs as soon as the ball is passed to 3 so 3 doesn't have the ball too long on the wing. This movement gives 3 a one-on-one opportunity.

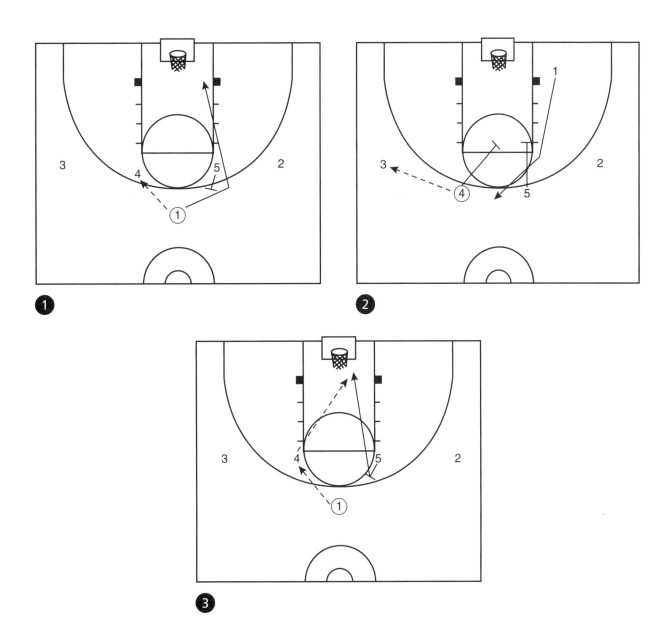

TRIPLE DOUBLE

Maria Fantanarosa

Objective

To get several three-point looks at the basket.

When to Use

- As a half-court inbounds play with several three-point threats against a man-to-man defense.
- In a continuity offense.

Key Personnel

You need a trio of three-point shooters and a team of fundamentally sound screeners.

Execution

1. 1 dribbles toward the left wing and then reverses and dribbles toward the right wing. 3 goes hard backdoor and continues off a stagger screen set by 2 and 5 to the wing and receives the pass from 1, looking to shoot (figure 1).

2. 1 and 4 set a double screen for 2, who pops to the top of the key for another three-point look (figure 2).

3. After 3 passes to 2, 3 sets a double screen with 5 for 4, who pops out to the wing for the third long-range look. 5 then seals in the post, and 3 pops to the top of the key (figure 3).

Variation

On the second double screen, 4 and 1 change their screening angles so 2 can flare to the left wing instead of popping to the top. This variation counters the defense's attempts to shoot the gap or achieve the guard-to-guard switch.

Points of Emphasis

This play takes 16 to 18 seconds to execute. The screens must be set tight and set continuously. Shooters must use and read the screens well.

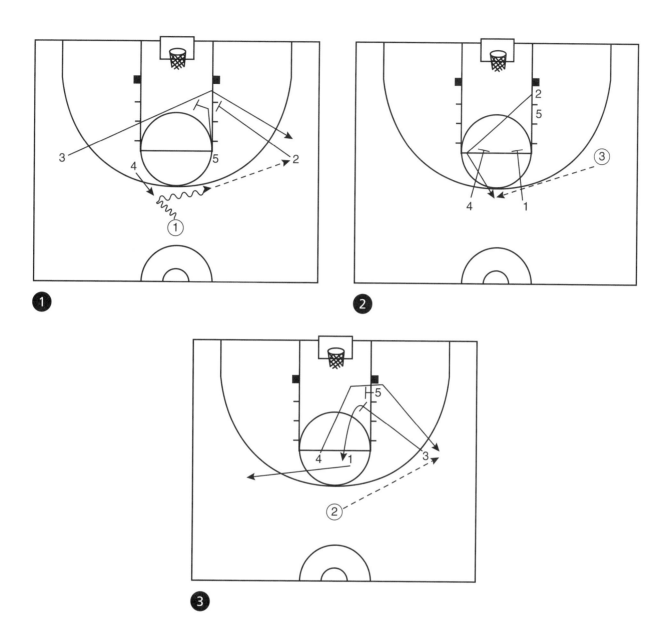

X

Maria Fantanarosa

Objective

To get a post player a high-percentage shot on the low block.

When to Use

As a half-court inbounds play against man-to-man defenses that struggle to defend multiple screens.

Key Personnel

You need a post who can finish inside and fundamentally sound guards.

Execution

1. 1 passes to 4 and then floats to the weak-side wing (figure 1).
2. 3 sets up for a backdoor cut but if not open after her first step receives the handoff from 4. 5 dives to just above the midpost area rim front to set the first of a stagger screen with 2. 1 replaces 2 on the wing (figure 2).
3. 4 drops to use the stagger screen as 3 immediately attacks the middle. If not open, she passes to 1, who looks for 4 posting up the on the low block (figure 3).

Variation

This variation can take advantage of a guard mismatch if the guard has post-up skills. The 4 fakes the handoff to 3 and instead reverses the ball to 1. 3 uses the stagger screen and posts her defender.

Points of Emphasis

This play takes 12 to 14 seconds to execute. The 2 and 5 must sprint to set up for the stagger screen. The 2 sets her second screen in front of the rim so 4 can receive the pass in ideal scoring position. The 3 reverses the ball before 4 comes off the last screen so 1 has time to hit 4 as soon as she's open. The 1 receives the pass at the elbow extended to create an ideal passing lane into 4. If 1 is denied, she should be open for a back door layup. If the post is a threat, the guards can get short jumpers immediately after the handoff.

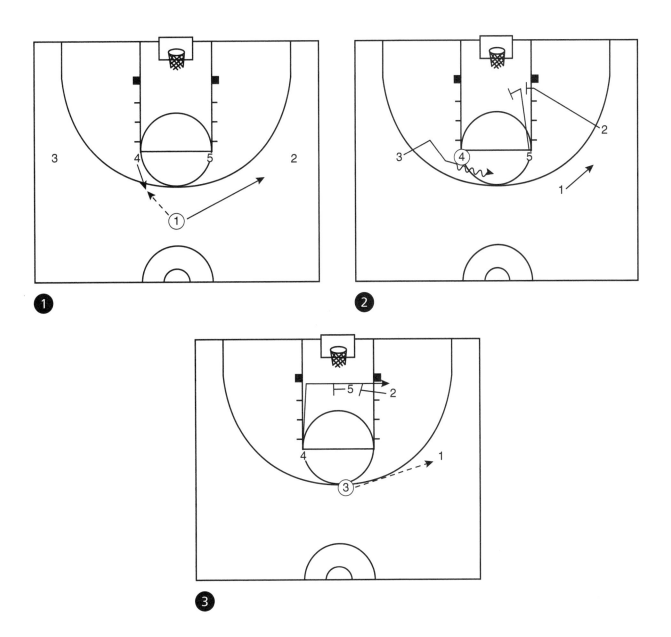

13

Tia Jackson

Objectives

- To isolate the point guard on the block or get a shooting guard open on the wing for a midrange jumper or three-pointer.
- To get more movement on offense and alleviate shots early in the shot clock.
- To hide ineffective post players.

When to Use

- Against teams that play a less-aggressive man-to-man defense.
- Also has pressure-release options against teams who full deny.

Key Personnel

Your 1 should be bigger than her defender and a hot shooter. Your 2 or 3 should be good at coming off screens. Your 5 should be comfortable handling the ball at the top of the key. Your 4 and 5 must set solid screens.

Execution

1. 1 dribbles to the left wing. 2 drops down to stack on the strong-side low block as 5 cuts high to receive the pass from 1 (figure 1).
2. When 5 has the ball, 3 cuts backdoor. If it's not there, 3 v-cuts to get open for the pass from 5 (figure 2).
3. On the pass to 3, 2 and 4 step out and set a double back screen for 1 cutting over the top, looking for a pass down low from 3. If 1 isn't open, 5 down-screens for 2 cutting off the double screen by 4 and 5 and 2 receives the pass from 3, looking for a shot (figure 3).
4. If no shot, 3 rubs off a screen by 1 on the strong-side block and then a double screen by 4 and 5 starting on the weak-side block. After 1 screens, she ducks into the lane. 2 passes to 1 or 3 (figure 4).

Variation

If 5's flash is denied when she flashes high, 1 can fake a pass to 5 at the top of the key and then hit her cutting backdoor.

Points of Emphasis

The play takes about 10 seconds to execute. The timing should be such that 1 is cutting to the block as the ball is being reversed to 3. The 1 must also remember to duck into the lane after her initial screen for 3 (a good option that tends to be overlooked).

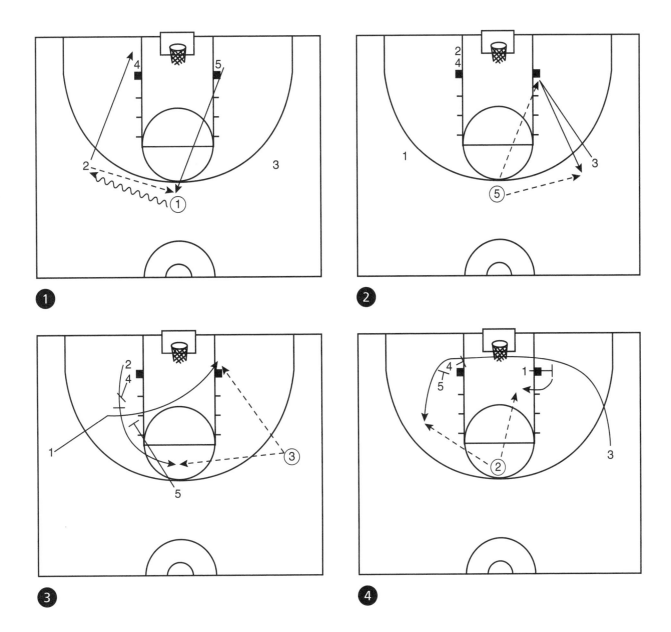

ISO

Tia Jackson

Objectives

- To get 2, 3, or a versatile 4 an opportunity to attack a slower defender using no more than two dribbles.
- To get a hot hand an easy look from 15 feet (4.5 m).

When to Use

- Against a man-to-man defense.
- When a defender is slow or in foul trouble.

Key Personnel

Your 2, 3, or 4 must possess more speed and quickness than her defender.

Execution

1. 1 passes to the post opposite the guard to be isolated, in this case 4. On the pass, 2 cuts to the strong-side corner as 5 dives to the ball-side block and 3 cuts up to the weak-side elbow (figure 1).

2. 4 passes to 3 near the elbow or, if 3 is overplayed, on a backdoor cut. Either way, 3 is now isolated and can take her defender one on one. 3 also can look for 5 on the seal inside before penetrating. If 3's defender denies the pass, 3 cuts back for a lob pass from 4 (figure 2).

Variation

Iso (short for isolation) can be run for a forward. In this case, 2 and 4 exchange spots, and 1 passes into 5 to initiate the play.

Points of Emphasis

The play takes about 8-10 seconds to execute. The player receiving the entry pass posts up on the elbow as she would on the block to get the pass from 1. The player on the block moves to open space as a relief option for 3.

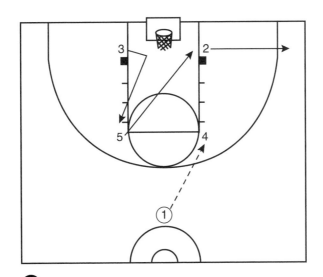

1

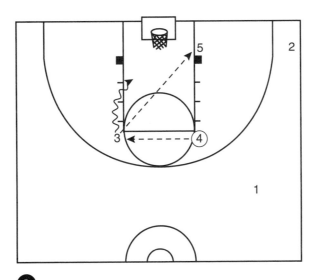

2

SHOOTER

Tia Jackson

Objective

To get a hot perimeter player, or a 4 with decent range, a good look within six seconds.

When to Use

Primarily against a man-to-man defense, although you can run the variation against a zone.

Key Personnel

Your 2 should be feeling confident with her shot and adept at using screens. Your 4 and 5 must be solid screeners, and 3 must be a threat from the perimeter in case the defenders switch.

Execution

1. 2 cuts to the middle of the key as 1 dribbles toward the baseline and back (figure 1).
2. 2 comes off a single screen by 3 or a double that includes 5, making the read to curl around 5, pop behind 5, or fade to the corner. Once 2 makes the read, 3 immediately cuts off a screen by 4 opposite 2 (figure 2).

Variation

Against a 2-3 zone, 3 and 5 screen the outside of the top and bottom of the zone. The 5 then seals the center of the zone after 3 flares off 4's screen. The 4 seals the center of the zone if 3 receives the pass.

Points of Emphasis

The 1 and 2 must read the curl, pop, or fade option correctly. The guards must set up their defenders in using the screens; the posts must set solid screens.

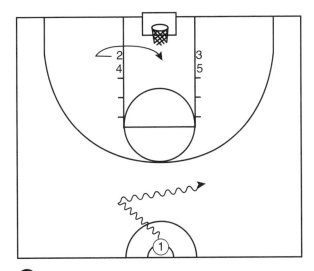

1

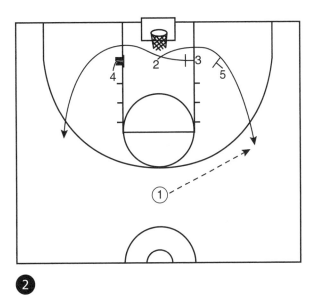

2

5-SECOND PLAY

Mary Taylor Cowles

Objectives

- To get the ball in a playmaker's hands with five to seven seconds left on the clock.
- To get a quick two- or three-pointer.

When to Use

- When the opponent is holding back on defense in fear of fouling.
- At the end of a game.

Key Personnel

Your passer must be intelligent and make good choices throwing the ball in. Your 1 is your best ball handler. Your two best shooters are at the far end of the court.

Execution

5 runs the baseline upon receiving the ball from the referee. 1 pops toward the ball and then uses 2's screen to get open on the wide wing. 5 hits 1 immediately, if open. If 1 is not open, 2 pops after the screen and catches the ball. 1 then plants and cuts down the middle of the floor to receive 2's pass. Depending on which defender helps on 1, 1 passes to 3 or 4 for the open three (figure 1).

Variation

If only a two-pointer is needed, a shooter can set up on the block and screen for the other shooter running to the opposite wing. The low-block shooter pins her defender in anticipation of the pass or to be in rebounding position (figure 2).

Points of Emphasis

This play is usually run at the end of a tight game when emotions are high. The 5 needs to take care not to rush the inbounds pass. The 1 and 2 should not rush the play. It takes only a few seconds to get the ball upcourt. The more time 5 can wait to ensure everyone is lined up, the better the play works. Coaches can help by having a substitution at the table on a dead-ball situation. If the game is tied or the offense is down by 3 points or less, the opposing coach is probably screaming at players not to foul. The 1 takes advantage of this by being very aggressive once the ball is in her hands. The two guards set up their defenders by running two to three steps opposite of where they really want to go.

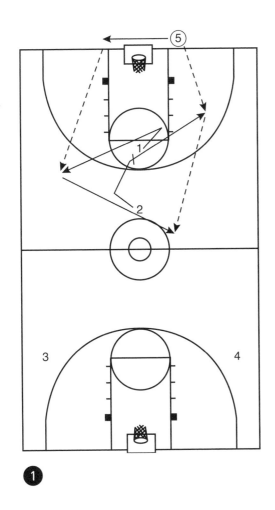

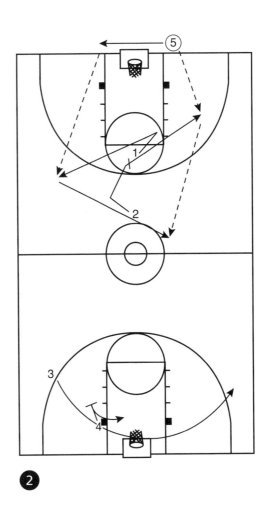

DRAGONS

Mary Taylor Cowles

Objective

To set up your best shooter for a three-point shot or your best playmaker for a one-on-one opportunity.

When to Use

- When a quick basket is needed.
- When a shooter has a hot hand.
- When an opponent cannot effectively guard the playmaker.

Key Personnel

Your 1 is your best playmaker and your 2 your best shooter. Your 4 should be the post player the opponent is most likely to sag off. Your 5 is your best inside scorer.

Execution

1. 1 dribbles to the shooter-side wing. 4 down-screens for 2, who pops up to the three-point line. 1 passes to 2. 5 then down-screens for 3, who gets open on the wing. 2 dribbles toward 3 and passes to her from the top of the key (figure 1).

2. 4 loops up to set a flare screen for 2. At the same time, 1 leaks toward the far-side block. As 3 passes to 2, 1 cross-screens for 5. 2 either takes the three-pointer or passes to 5 (figure 2).

3. 3 and 4 then set a stagger screen for 1 coming to the top of the key (figure 3).

Variation

The 1 and 2 switch places to begin the play to set up a great one-on-one opportunity for 1 and puts 2 at the top of the key at the end of the play for another option.

Points of Emphasis

This play takes about 10 seconds to execute. Timing and setup are key. The 5 must time her down screen for 3 until the ball is passed to shooter. The 3 must get open or the flare screen is taken away. The 2 gets to the top of the key before reaching the flare screen. Otherwise, she'll be limited in the space she has to work with. The 1 is on the block when 2 is coming off her screen so 1's defender can't help on 2. The 2 and the weaker post should be on the side from which 2 is most comfortable taking shots.

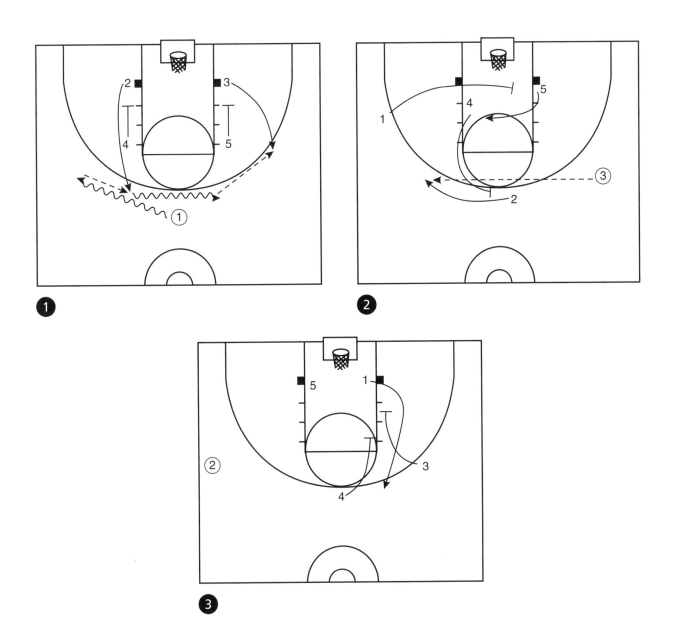

GEORGETOWN

Mary Taylor Cowles

Objective

To get your best shooter open.

When to Use

- When a quick three-pointer or play to the best post is needed.
- Out of a set or as a secondary break.
- The variation can be used as an out-of-bounds play.

Key Personnel

Your 1 and 4 must set good screens. Your 5 must do a good job hunting and wanting the ball. Your shooter (2) must have great range and accuracy, read the defense well, and work hard to get open.

Execution

1 starts on the left side and reverses the ball to 4. 4 looks for 5 hunting the ball and then reverses to 3 as 5 continues to hunt the ball. 2 starts toward the basket and then cuts back up to use a stagger screen by 1 and 4 to get to the top of the key for the pass from 3 (see the figure).

Variations

- If 4 isn't open on the reversal, 1 skips the ball to 3.
- As a sideline out-of-bounds play, 1 inbounds to 4 popping out to start the play.

Points of Emphasis

This play takes about seven seconds to execute. The post working inside for the ball is key to this play. By having action on the opposite side, the post should have a one-one-one opportunity. If the defense goes under the screen, the shooter (2) should flare. If the defender rides 2 off, 2 needs to be comfortable curling. The 1 and 4 should read their defenders on the screen and be ready to slip, if possible.

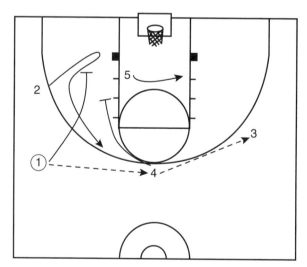

GREENWOOD

Mary Taylor Cowles

Objective

To throw the ball as far upcourt as possible to the best playmaker for a quick shot.

When to Use

- In late-game situations with a few seconds on the clock, especially when the opponent is worried about fouling.
- Can be used for a quick two-pointer or three-pointer.

Key Personnel

Your passer (3) is a strong, accurate passer and intelligent player who makes good decisions late in the game. Your 1 is your best playmaker. Your shooter (5) is your best shooter. Your 2 should also be a good shooter and someone who recognizes when to come back to the ball if necessary. Your 4 should be the best rebounder and rim player.

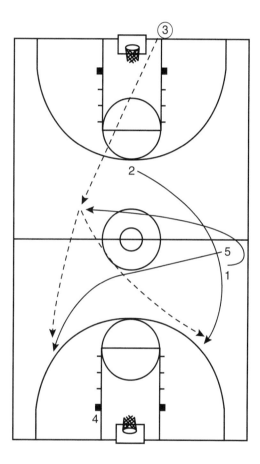

Execution

Stack the shooter and playmaker (5 and 1) at midcourt. 2 takes off in a dead sprint toward the stack. The shooter curls to the far corner, and 1 curls off 2 to the deepest area to which the passer can accurately throw it. The passer (3) hits 1, who immediately looks for the shooter in the corner for a quick three or for 2 running to the opposite wing. The 2 cuts back to the ball if 1 is not open (see the figure).

Points of Emphasis

It's almost imperative to run this play after a time-out or free-throw in order to get players lined up properly. The passer can't be afraid to lead 1 with the ball and let her go get it. Remind players that three seconds is plenty of time to catch, look for the shooter, and get a shot off.

TIGER

Lisa Stone

Objectives

- To set up multiple options for a quick hit.
- To give an athletic point guard a chance to catch and finish a lob pass.

When to Use

When the opponent is actively pressuring the point guard and the 5 draws attention from the defense.

Key Personnel

Your 1 is athletic enough to catch a lob and finish. Your 5 is an effective scorer who draws the defense's attention. Your 4 is a great screener who can knock down open shots.

Execution

4 down-screens for 3, who pops out to the wing, while the shooter (2) sprints to the corner and 5 dives to the ball-side block. 1 passes to 3 and then rubs off a back screen by 4 to get open for the lob. If 4's defender helps with 1, 4 pops out for the open shot (see the figure).

Variation

If the defenders of 1 and 4 switch on the screen, maintain good positioning and take advantage of the post guarding 1 by running 1 to the wing to get open and attack.

Points of Emphasis

This play takes about 10 seconds to execute. Timing is critical. If the shooter's cut, 4's down screen, and 5's dive don't all happen at the same time, the point guard won't be alone for the lob. The 5 diving to the block and 2 running to the corner is the first option. If 5 draws enough attention, 1 should be open if 4 sets a good screen.

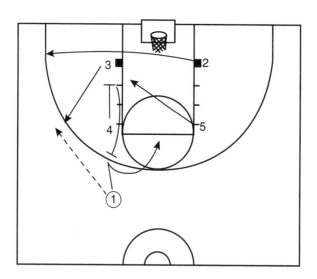

DOUBLE SCREEN HIGH

Lisa Stone

Objectives

- To get your point guard into the paint to make a play.
- To get a three-point look.

When to Use

- As a quick hit, as the shot clock or game clock is winding down, or as a late game situation.
- Against a man-to-man defense.

Key Personnel

Your 1 must be a solid ball handler, capable of dribble penetration off the ball screen. Your 3 must be a threat from long-range. Your 4 must set good screens.

Execution

1 dribbles toward the left elbow and then uses a double screen by 2 and 4 to reverse and penetrate to the basket or looks to pass to 3 or 5. If no one's open, 1 passes to 2, who gets open using 4's cross- or down screen (see the figure).

Points of Emphasis

This play takes 10 to 12 seconds (or less) to execute. It's important for all players to be a threat, and dribble penetration is crucial. The 1 must do a good job using the screen and attacking the basket in hopes of drawing a defender, creating a dish to an open shooter. If the 4's defender is worried for the shooter, 4 slips down to create a high-low opportunity between 4 and 5. The 2 sets up closest to the basket.

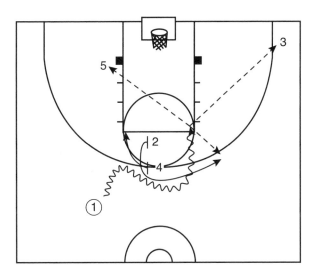

SCREEN 4-3

Lisa Stone

Objectives

- To capitalize on a guard-post mismatch.
- To get an open look at a three-point shot.

When to Use

- Against a man-to-man defense that switches on screens.
- When a shooter is on a roll.

Key Personnel

Your 1 should be a strong ball-handling guard. Your 2 needs good range and must be comfortable shooting off a screen.

Execution

1. If 2 is the primary shooter, 1 dribbles toward and then passes to 3. 1 then screens for 4 and widens out to the right wing while 2 cuts hard backdoor and stays on the right block (figure 1).

2. 3 passes to 4, who completes the ball reversal by swinging it to 1. Immediately upon 1 receiving the ball, 2 sets a back screen for 3, who cuts hard to the right block (figure 2).

3. 5 and 4 set a stagger screen for 2, who looks for the three-point shot (figure 3).

Variation

If the defense decides to switch, look to capitalize on the mismatch. For instance, if 2's defender switches to 5 after 5 screens 2 (figure 4), 3 should cut to the strong-side corner, which allows 5 to dive to the right block and post up a guard.

Points of Emphasis

This play usually takes 10 to 12 seconds to execute. Setting solid screens is an obvious key. An effective outside shooter allows for guard dribble penetration because the weak-side defender is too worried about the shooter cutting off the stagger screen. If the offense is losing movement when the defense switches on screen, get the ball to a dominant post player on the block. This play is fun to run because it allows the offense to be creative in reading how the defense is reacting to the play by using dribble penetration and screen slips.

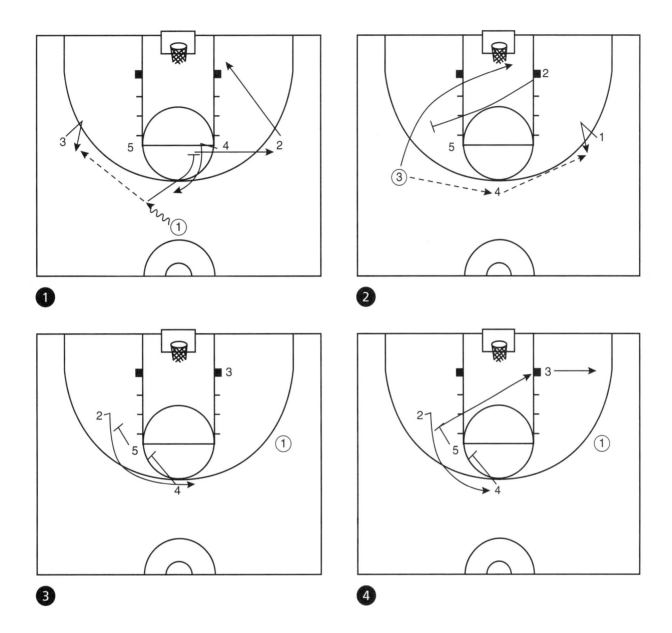

ABOUT THE WBCA

Founded in 1981, the **Women's Basketball Coaches Association (WBCA)** promotes women's basketball by unifying coaches at all levels to develop a reputable identity for the sport of women's basketball and fosters and promotes the development of the game in all of its aspects as a sport for women and girls.

With members throughout the world, it is the largest organization of its kind. The WBCA is involved in a variety of events and clinics throughout the year, including the WBCA High School All-America Game; the Betty F. Jaynes Internship Program; the Nike So You Want To Be A Coach Program; and the annual WBCA National Convention, held in conjunction with the NCAA Women's Final Four. Through these events, the WBCA not only highlights exceptionally talented female players but also provides opportunities for coaches at all levels to better themselves.

In addition to the activities that the WBCA puts on and sponsors, the organization has an extensive awards program through which the best, brightest, and most talented athletes, coaches, and contributors to women's basketball are honored. The WBCA also provides coverage on all aspects of women's basketball, from high school to the pros, through their three publications: *Coaching Women's Basketball*, *Net.News*, and *Compliance Corner*.

For more information on these and the many activities and opportunities available from the WBCA, check out www.wbca.org.

CONTRIBUTORS

The following are coaches who contributed to *WBCA Offensive Play & Strategies*:

- Agnus Berenato, University of Pittsburgh
- Gary Blair, Texas A&M University
- Lisa Bluder, University of Iowa
- Doug Bruno, DePaul University
- Beth Burns, San Diego State University
- Van Chancellor
- Tom Collen, University of Arkansas
- Mary Taylor Cowles, Western Kentucky University
- June Daugherty, Washington State University
- Maria Fantanarosa, Miami University of Ohio
- Sylvia Hatchell, University of North Carolina
- Quentin Hillsman, Syracuse University
- Tom Hodges, Morehead State University
- Rick Insell, Middle Tennessee State University
- Tia Jackson
- MaChelle Joseph, Georgia Tech University
- Felisha Legette-Jack, Indiana University
- Cristy McKinney
- Kathy Miller
- Matthew Mitchell, University of Kentucky
- Deb Patterson, Kansas State University
- Jennifer Rizzotti, University of Hartford
- Audra Smith, University of Alabama at Birmingham
- Lisa Stone
- Charli Turner Thorne, Arizona State University
- Jeff Walz, University of Louisville